INFLUENCE
With A Heart

How To Be A Better Leader and Communicator by Using More Empathy, Story, and Thought Leadership

(So You Can Make A Bigger Impact, Make More Money, and Help More People)

Ben Gioia

Influence With A Heart
How To Be A Better Leader and Communicator by
Using More Empathy, Story, and Thought Leadership

What People Are Saying About Ben Gioia and His Strategies

*"Ben Gioia is changing business for the better through what he teaches. I truly believe that his insights about **influential communication and leadership** will support those people — who have ideas and strategies proven to help transform the world — to **brand and package** what they offer for distribution on a larger scale."*

—Kathleen L. Keller, PhD Mark T. Greenberg Professor
for the Study of Children's Health and Development
Assistant Professor in the Department(s) of
Nutritional Sciences and Food Science
Pennsylvania State University

*"Ben is a coach, author, speaker, and seminar leader who truly cares about making a positive difference in the lives of others. In addition, he is a **very smart businessperson** who can tremendously **help you grow your business.** It is my sincere honor to introduce you to Ben Gioia!"*

—James Malinchak
Featured on the ABC Hit TV Show, "Secret Millionaire"
The World's #1 Speaker Trainer
Founder, BigMoneySpeaker.com

*"Thank you, Ben, for your **insights and recommendations.** Your ideas are very helpful and align well with my strategic plan. I'm so grateful for you as a 'trusted adviser.'"*

—Laurence Hansen
Executive Coach: Friend & Champion

*"What resonates the most with me about Ben is his **heartfelt and patient** approach, blended with **skillful coaching aimed at achieving results**. Ben offers an array of ideas, resources, and a strategic plan that gives traction to your vision while staying connected to the heart of your business."*

—Annette Segal
CEO and Founder, The Valiant Group
Executive and Leadership Coaching

*"I have known Ben for several years, and I can unhesitatingly say that he is **the "real deal."** Ben applies the same principles of honesty, empathy, and authenticity (while offering a **powerful skill set**)... whether he's helping a client deliver their product or service, coaching someone on reshaping their career, or helping leaders articulate and bring their vision and message to the world.*

*"I have benefited immensely from Ben's ideas and guidance about **open communication, ethical influence, thought leadership, and building trust** with my intended audience... by sharing personal and professional stories. "Ben practices what he preaches: consciousness, consistency, and authenticity — and applies them to **sustainable business growth, personal success, and inner harmony.** No wonder he is a successful speaker, coach, author, and communications guru!"*

—Amit Satsangi, MBA
Unravelling the Growth Story
Hidden In Your Customer Data (Analytics)

"Starting a new business is hard at any age, but it was especially daunting for me, because I had worked for

corporations for 30+ years. Going out of my comfort zone meant taking risks, and it was great to have Ben to bounce ideas off. **Ben gave me useful tools** and ways to think about what services I had to offer and how I could **position my business in an effective and marketable way.**"

—Ann Powell, Director, Responsive Edit
Former Managing Editor of *AARP The Magazine*
(One of the largest in the world (circulation 32 million))

"The road less taken can often be the smartest, especially long term, if it leads to a win-win. Almost anyone can do a one-shot sale. It takes a leader to make it sustainable. **Thanks to you, Ben, for your valuable insights...** *to build relationships that last, and a profitable, sustainable, competitive business in the process."*

—George H. Schofield, PhD
Author, Speaker Expert on High Quality Life
After 50 It's Up To Us, GeorgeSchofield.com

"Ben helped me understand two things: I was undercharging (thereby not allowing talented people to believe I was qualified to coach them) and that I should realize that I just needed to be a resource. The latter was **a shift in my consciousness:** *just give, be kind, be helpful, be a resource, and stop worrying about selling. It worked!* **I'm thrilled** *to be working with the clients who trust me and am excited about creating transformation with the change agents I now attract.* **Ben helped me up my game** *— so that I can better serve the world. Doesn't get much better!"*

—Kenji Oshima, CPCC, ACC
Coaching High Performing Entrepreneurs and Leaders

"Ben **helped me to clarify a bigger vision** of my goals. He is extremely skilled and sensitive in the listening and dialogue process, which allows him to grasp the direction the client is going and to delve deeper into their true vision by asking the right questions."

—Sonia Perel, MA
Yoga Therapist for Individuals,
Organizations, and Mental Health Professionals

"Ben is an incredibly talented coach. His partnership has helped me to quickly deliver several critical elements of my brand and positioning that I had been challenged to accurately produce on my own. **I highly recommend Ben—** if you're an organization, entrepreneur, or change agent that's looking for a heart-based collaborative partner to represent, elevate, and **best express your authentic message...** with power, heart, and profound clarity."

—Steve Havill, CEO, Change Agent
Conscious Business Consultant
Certified High Performance Coach

"Ben, thank you. You have an awesome mind for grasping someone's business or talent and assisting them to understand **the marketing, influence, and leadership principles to make this a reality.** You seized upon my talents and brought these to the fore so it changed the whole focus of my unique positioning and offer... brilliant! I will certainly recommend you as a coach and trainer."

—Dave Stone, Speaker, Author
Founder Mindful Mentoring
Founder, Guru Marketing

*"I asked Ben to help with the **launch of my book.** His expertise and wealth of ideas let me know I was in very good hands, and his empathetic, down-to-earth nature **put me immediately at ease.** Working with Ben demystified my marketing, while reassuring me that I don't have to do it all alone! I enthusiastically recommend that other holistic entrepreneurs do the same!"*

—Mikki Baloy Davis
Intuitive, Teacher, and Shamanic Healer,
Author of *Hallowed Underground:
Sacred Hope & Healing in Dark Times*

*"Ben is a great partner. He knows how to support you while pushing/challenging you to be better. His **expertise in the influence/communications** arena showed up time and time again in our work together. I encourage you to **talk to Ben** if you are looking for guidance and/or support in making a bigger impact and utilizing communications as a key tool to get your message out into the world."*

—Mike Normant
Trainer/Coach/Consultant
Helping People Lead More Fulfilling Lives

*"I love Ben's framework and appreciate how he offers tons of value instead of trying to 'close a sale'. Because of his philosophy on serving others, **I'm excited to recommend him** to other entrepreneurs who are looking to be more influential with their message! An incredible speaker and coach, countless people benefit from him and his teaching!"*

—Jason Rogers
Founder of PEAK Inc.

"I met Ben Gioia when he was the Marketing Director for the Bay Area Conscious Capitalism chapter. I knew his heart was in the right place. There was a sense of sincerity and authenticity about him that **inspired me** to seek out his guidance.

"I was re-positioning my business and wanted to get his take on being truly conscious about it. Ben's ideas were **lucid, strategic** and **insightful,** all focused on helping me communicate **my vision,** thinking bigger and keeping a keen eye on my **customers' needs** and concerns. Something in particular really stuck: an idea he had for **illuminating my 'special sauce.'"**

—Leslie Lawton
Inspired Branding, Web & Mobile
Copywriter & Content Marketing Strategist

"Ben offered a wise, listening ear when I was faced with an unexpected opportunity to **transform my personal brand and take my career in a new direction.** His thoughtful questions and insightful feedback crystallized what my intuition had been telling me: to fully align my professional skills and expertise with my personal mission to be a force for good, and catalyze meaningful positive change. **Inspired by Ben's coaching,** I found the position I love!"

—Catherine Goerz
Communications Strategist
PR, Marketing & Branding Maven
Global Tech and Communications for Salesfore.com

(from the offices of)
Influence With A Heart
San Francisco, CA, USA

Hi it's Ben,

Thanks for being here and reading this book. It's an honor to share this with you. You're about to receive so much value in the following pages. (I'm so excited!)

But, there's so much more that's not in this book, simply because it won't fit. More valuable writing, videos, audios, and trainings... which are all available to you (at no cost) at influencewithaheart.com.

SO, LET'S STAY IN TOUCH!

I invite you to take a look, find what you like, and subscribe to my list. When you do this, I can keep bringing you the most current, proven methods, tools, and strategies that will help you be even more successful in your business and make a bigger impact.

Thanks for doing what you do!

Cheers,

Ben

influencewithaheart.com

Ben's First Book, The #1 Best Seller

"This is a must read for any salesperson, business owner, or entrepreneur. **Marketing With A Heart: How To Use Trust Based Marketing For Greater Income, Influence, and Impact** *is not just about marketing and selling. It is about communicating with people. Ben shares his incredible heartfelt experiences and principles to help build lasting relationships in any business. I am recommending this book to all of my clients."*

—John Formica
An "Ex-Disney Guy", Speaker and Author
America's Customer Experience Coach

Nearly 40 Case Studies provide real examples of Ben's teachings and how they can be most effectively applied to different businesses, organizations, and movements. Get it here (print or digital): amazon.com/author/bengioia

"Coaches, consultants, teachers, and leaders with a message of service... read this book and join me in following Ben's lead. Together we can elevate and enlighten the practice of reaching out and offering our gifts and talents to those whom we are meant to serve."

—Lou D'Alo, Founder of PowerUpCoaching.com
Marketing for Enlightened Business Owners

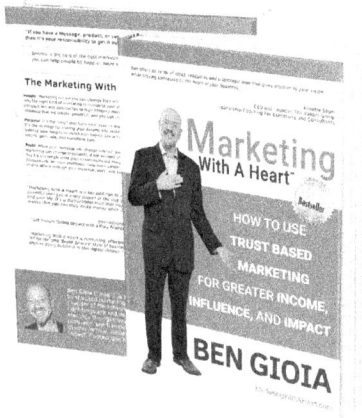

Did You Know?

Your ability to make an even bigger impact in the world happens when you:

1) Express your unique purpose;

2) Communicate with empathy; and

3) Tell your story while maximizing & leveraging your thought leadership, positioning, and influence.

• *MARKETING WITH A HEART* will help you do this... whether you're an executive, entrepreneur, small business owner, speaker, leader, author, coach, consultant, or other visionary. You will become a better communicator and a more influential leader.

This #1 best seller is available in print, on your favorite devices, and is ready for purchase in Australia, Brazil, Canada, China, France, Germany, India, Italy, Japan, Mexico, the Netherlands, Spain, and the United Kingdom. amazon.com/author/bengioia

"No matter the industry — for any of us to make bigger impact — we need to present ourselves bigger, brighter, and bolder than ever before. We need to pump up the volume: how we present and use our authority, thought leadership, and influence. Let's do it in a way that creates connection and trust, while building lasting relationships!"
                                                             —Ben Gioia

For Alia... with so much love, gratitude, and delight!

Foreword

For a man who escaped death 4 times in 72 hours, Ben Gioia looks pretty good! As a medical doctor, that's my professional opinion.

(I'll let him share the rest of that *powerful story* with you… and how it changed his life.)

Meanwhile, I will say that Ben Gioia doesn't seem to miss a moment. Or a word. Or an action. He gives so much **focus, presence, love, and care** to everything he does… whether he's speaking to a group, working one-on-one with his clients, or composing the words for this book.

I have the sneaking suspicion that his "loving attention" may have come from his being given a second chance at life (as well a third, a fourth, AND a fifth chance)!

Ben is the master of putting things together in a way that creates synergy, efficiency, and transformation. Where **leadership, influence, communication, and service** intersect, no one else can touch him. He is unique, and one the best.

Ben Gioia speaks, trains, and coaches like a conductor leads an orchestra. He unites the instruments of influence together in exquisite harmonies, creating an entire symphony of inspired action which shows people how to be better leaders and better communicators so they can make an even more significant and positive impact in the world.

In his second book, *Influence With A Heart,* Ben Gioia has done it again, this time leading you **step-by-step** to the surprising conclusion that influence isn't something that you do TO people... it's actually something that you do FOR people. (In Steven Covey's words of wisdom, this is the "win-win.")

The great value of this book? You can apply the teachings to your business and to your life immediately. It will impact you long before you reach the last chapter, and will continue long after.

Ben often says that he is not really making any new suggestions. Instead, he is simply blessed to have the opportunity to pass along the knowledge he has learned (and the wisdom he's cultivated)... thanks to the visionaries, leaders, and masters that came before him.

He may be a little modest in this regard. He certainly **offers perspectives and tools that are new to me,** and many of them will clearly make a difference in how I communicate with my staff, patients, and colleagues... as well as how I drive new initiatives in my organization.

I found that even some of his seemingly more "common" success teachings are under-appreciated and under-used in my own life.

And the concepts that I thought I understood — the ones I personally know and use — were presented to me in new, clearer ways that made them even easier to apply *and* profoundly more practical.

And "practical" just about sums it up: the insights, teachings, and tools from *Influence With A Heart* will work for you, regardless of your industry or area of expertise.

(After you read it once, I suggest you read it again.)

Ben Gioia has sat at the feet of some very influential teachers, **helped to launch one of the biggest magazines in the world, trained business leaders at Stanford, helped position a million dollar global brand, positively impacted half of the people in California with ALS** (Lou Gehrig's disease), and so much more.

Now as an author, speaker, coach, and consultant, his influence is even greater.

Why? Because he helps good people around the world — who are doing good things — make an even bigger impact.

So when you tap into the expertise and wisdom of Ben Gioia, you will receive much more than you may expect.

You are learning from a person whose life purpose (inspired by the words of Buckminster Fuller) is to help, *"Make things work, for everyone and everything, as quickly as possible, through compassionate action, without hurting people or exploiting the planet."*

This powerful book offers a generous display of some of Ben's many gifts, talents, and a better way to do business.

This is a **great, valuable, and game-changing** read!

—Dr. Dane Treat, M.D.
Regional Medical Director, CareATC
A Proactive Approach To Workforce Health
Phoenix, Arizona, US

Table of Contents

Why This Book Is Right On Time

This is an amazing time in history. Entrepreneurs, organizations, leaders, and visionaries are helping to move humanity forward and enhance life for more people, both today and for many generations down the line. To do this, they're creating and growing amazing businesses, movements, and positive social change.

Why is this happening? Because more and more people are realizing that everyone and everything on this planet are interconnected. So the impact — these people are making — is both worldwide and one-to-one.

• Now, imagine if each one of these people — had more power to **inspire more people to say, "yes"** — to their ideas, vision, message, products, and/or services…

• Imagine if each one of these people — could quickly and easily be more influential — so they can reach more people, cultivate more win-win relationships, achieve more results, be more successful, and set a positive example for other businesses and leaders…

• Now, imagine what happens when all of these people — "turn up the volume" on their **influence, impact, and income** — so they can help more people, whether it's one, or 10, or 10,000 more people…

Making A Bigger Impact In Your World

If you're like me, you want to make a bigger impact in the world. And if you think about it... making a bigger impact comes down to one key thing: using more influence in every aspect of your **communication and leadership.**

Because when you use more influence — and do it ethically — you inspire more people to take action that's **good for them** *and* **good for you** (win-win). This means more success for you and your organization or business.

That's what *Influence With A Heart* is all about.

When you use more influence, more people will:

1. Find you and connect with you;

2. Sign up for your list;

3. Follow you on social media and share your message;

4. Purchase your products;

5. Invest in your services;

6. Invite you into their boardrooms, onto their webinars, or onto their stages; and

7. Give you the opportunity to lead them or help them… so they can create more success and impact with their business, in their workplace, or in their life.

Using more influence is a simple, effective way to become a better leader and communicator… while using your business or organization to make real, positive change happen (today, and as part of your legacy for the future).

You can use more influence anywhere, anytime, with anyone including:

1. when you're face-to-face, on the phone, recording a video, writing an email, creating a product, running a meeting, delivering a service, or speaking to an audience;

2. during your speech, webinar, or training… so you can inspire more people, give them a new perspective, and show them powerful and positive next steps on the road to their success;

3. in your day-to-day expression, example, and articulation of your unique style of leadership… so you can move yourself, your team, or your organization into action;

4. on your website… so the right people will be engaged, read your content, and join your list;

5. within your emails… so people will open, read, and click to take action;

6. in your LinkedIn summary… so the opportunities — that you want — will come your way; and

7. during your discovery call or on your sales page… so you can get more clients or customers, make more money, and make a bigger impact.

In a nutshell, if you want to **make more success happen — in your company, organization, or world —** it's critical that you become a better communicator and a more influential leader.

Why? Because your clients, customers, colleagues, and/ or audience need to get inspired and excited about who you are and what you offer, so they can take action.

Whether you're a leader, expert, authority, or thought leader, people must understand that you are authentic, that you understand them, and that you care.

• • •

Think of it like this: **influence *(with a heart)* is simply the art of inspiring people** to take action that's good for them and good for you, so you can make a bigger impact.

How To Use This Book and What To Expect

What you'll find in the pages of *Influence With A Heart* can be applied to multiple aspects of your business and your life: by helping you to communicate more effectively, be a better leader, and make a bigger impact in the world.

You're about to **discover concepts, perspectives,** and strategies about leadership and communication that you can use, model, and share with others, right away.

The methods are presented in a clear, simple, and direct way, so you'll have no doubt about how and when to use your new **insights, wisdom, and strategies.**

This isn't like any other book you've read.

• It's saturated with takeaways (that can be applied by every person in every field and industry).

• It's based on proven methods and timeless principles that have been used by masters, orators, writers, innovators, experts, visionaries, and leaders throughout history… and will continue into the future.

• Although it's a nonfiction book, I've written it as an unconventional narrative that's conversational and filled with stories, imagery, anecdotes, provocative questions, action steps, humor, case studies, and multiple opportunities for you to reflect, learn, and take action.

What I'm offering **in this book is a framework** for being a better communicator and a more influential leader.

My intention is that you take what you learn (plus the wisdom you cultivate and the insights you experience) and create the success, income, and impact you want.

You're about to **discover a better way to do business** and practical steps that you can take to make it happen. I wish you every possible success, and more!

So I invite you to take a few moments to be here and be present, so you can get the most out of what's inside.

Shut the door, put your phone in airplane mode, and get comfy…

Take a few deep, nourishing breaths…

Have a notebook handy, get some sticky notes, scribble in the margins, dictate your thoughts into your phone, and capture your discoveries…

As I tell you a little story… about *Influence With A Heart*.

Your Mission: Inspiring More People To Say, "Yes" To Your Ideas, Vision, Message, Product, or Service

Take a look at history and take a look at what's happening in our world, right now.

Influence is powerful stuff.

In the wrong hands and used the wrong ways, influence can be dangerous to your health, happiness, safety, spirituality, dignity, legacy, and freedom.

But in **the right hands (like yours),** just imagine what can happen when influence is used the right way!

By communicating with more influence, you inspire more people to take action. More people will say, "yes" to you.

And remember: **this is your one, single mission**… no matter what. This is the one thing — that absolutely must happen — for you to succeed. Your entire business hinges on this.

You must inspire more people to say, "yes."

You want to inspire people to say, "yes" to what you offer... so you can impact their lives.

When you do this, more people will have the opportunity to **have their business or life transformed** by who you are and what you bring to the table. (Not just the people today, but those who will be impacted by your legacy.)

Depending on your industry, role, and/or position, there are lots of important, **powerful, valuable ways that people can (and will) say, "yes" to you.**

10 of the "big ones" are:

1. Choosing to visit your website, subscribing to your list, and opening your emails.

2. Clicking on your call-to-action, joining your webinar, and buying your book, training, or product.

3. Connecting with you on LinkedIn and/or contacting you for an interview.

4. Hiring you for a leadership position or consultancy.

5. Inviting you to speak or train (onstage and/or online).

6. Offering you a partnership or an appointment.

7. Investing in your services or events.

8. Doing your marketing for you… by referring you to their colleagues, clients, and community.

9. Signing up for your coaching or leadership program.

10. (If you're a leader, manager, or part of a team) "yes" happens via higher engagement, retention, loyalty, innovation, and productivity.

Which of these 10 "big ones" apply to you?

No matter who you are and what you do, these 10 "big ones"… these 10 "yeses" are so important because they will help move your business forward… fast.

<u>It all starts by using more empathy, story, and thought leadership, whether you're face-to-face, online, onstage, or on the phone.</u>

You'll automatically use more influence, every time you communicate. You'll inspire and invite more people to say, "yes"… to making a choice that's good for them and good for you. (Whether it's opening your email, joining your presentation, or joining your team.)

Whether you're an entrepreneur, visionary, or leader… just imagine how many lives you can impact with your ideas, message, vision, product, or service!

This Is How Influence (With A Heart) Works

(*more*) Empathy +
(*more*) Story +
(*more*) Thought Leadership = **Influence With A Heart™**

• **Empathy** gives you the opportunity to see the world through another person's eyes. It creates connection and is the foundation for relationships based on trust.

• **Stories** create inspiration and an emotional experience for your reader or listener because they reach people's hearts as well as their minds.

• **Thought leadership** is how you're known for making a difference in your business, organizations, and/or in your world… with your innovative ideas and perspectives.

The strategies and framework you learn in *Influence With A Heart* will help people know, like, and trust you… while positioning you as a caring expert, authority, or thought leader… who can connect the dots — from what people want and need — to who you are and what you offer.

You can use this framework **anytime, anywhere, with anyone:** in person, online, onstage, on the phone, in a training, in a video, during a speech, or in a meeting.

A Quick Hello

My name is Ben Gioia ("joya") and I show people how to be better leaders and more influential communicators so they can make a bigger impact, make more money, and help more people.

I'm a speaker, coach, trainer, and author of the #1 best-selling book *Marketing With A Heart: How To Use Trust Based Marketing For Greater Income, Influence, and Impact.* I've presented to audiences (onstage and online) around the country and around the world (groups of 5 to conferences of 500+).

My second book, *Influence With A Heart* (which you're reading right now), will teach you how to inspire more of your clients, customers, colleagues, and audience — so **they will say, "yes" to your ideas, vision, messages, products, or service** — whether you're communicating face-to-face, online, onstage, or on the phone.

In this book, I'm going to share the same tools, techniques, strategies, and perspectives that I used to make these 7 things happen:

1. **Position** Right Mission, Right Money (a global brand that trains social entrepreneurs) and help add almost **$1 million** to the founder's bottom line.

2. Launch one of the **biggest magazines in the world:** *AARP The Magazine* (32 million circulation).

3. **Train 126 top leaders at Stanford University,** for two days, in influential communication, leadership, and positioning. Speak to global business leaders about empathy and story at the University of Washington.

4. **Create the marketing strategy** for a San Francisco nonprofit during Phase 2 of its launch which increased membership by 37% and sponsorship by 30%.

5. **Facilitate an organizational consolidation** for The ALS Association between the Los Angeles and San Francisco chapters. By combining two Chapters, the organization could now serve 50% of the people in California with Lou Gehrig's disease.

6. Guide a boutique technology company in **rebranding and repositioning** to attract more social impact business (Bay Area and Silicon Valley). The company has helped UCSF Medical Center improve healthcare delivery for people with AIDS and also created an app that helps farmers irrigate their crops for best results.

7. Help a high-end executive coach take her business online and **attract even more major clients** such as Cisco, Twitter, and NASA.

These **same tools, techniques, strategies, and perspectives** that I used (for these 7 successes) are what you can expect to learn throughout this book.

I also have a powerful story to share.

During a hike in India, I almost died. *4 times… in 72 hours!* (More on this later.)

Those 72 hours gave me a profound gratitude for life and a fire inside to create massive, positive impact.

First, I created and launched Marketing With A Heart™. Then I created and launched Influence With A Heart™.

I'm grateful to help people speak, write, and present themselves (and their business) — in a way that inspires positive action in the world around them.

I'm delighted that you're here right now and reading these words. May they support your happiness, success, and your ability to make a bigger impact and leave a legacy that will continue to help people!

(If what I'm sharing resonates, and you want to chat, I invite you to visit InfluenceWithAHeart.com/contact.)

The 7 Characteristics of Great
Leaders and Influential Communicators

There are lots of ways to think about leadership and being a leader.

For the sake of what you're discovering in this book, I'll use this as a working definition:

• **Leadership** *is the combination and expression of presence, integrity, insight, communication, and action… that allows individuals or organizations to "lead," guide, or influence other individuals, groups, teams, or organizations.*

In my years of leadership roles in the magazine world, with a major US nonprofit, and then as a speaker, coach, author, and entrepreneur — supported by reading lots of books, studying, and learning from amazing coaches and mentors — I've identified 7 characteristics of great leaders and influential communicators.

1. **Go-To People** They are reliable sources of information and the go-to people in their field of expertise.

2. **Make Connections** They're able to connect — both who they are and what they offer — to the outcomes that people want.

3. **Inspirational** They inspire others with new points of view, stories, and innovative ideas. They turn these ideas into success and offer a blueprint or roadmap for others to replicate that success.

4. **Relationships** They create authentic rapport thanks to their excellent interpersonal skills and humility, plus their ability to give and receive feedback, skillfully.

5. **Reach, Response, and Results** They're good at building networks that are based on trust and continually expanding their sphere of influence by inspiring others.

6. They are **Creative** (instead of competitive) which contributes to their personal wellbeing, effective, communication, and unparalleled leadership. They express their unique purpose in a way that helps their business to succeed.

7. **Game Changers** They are known for making a difference in their work, for the people who are impacted by their business, and in their world.

In addition to my direct experience, this list has been informed by some of the best insights, teaching, and real life examples from Steven Covey, Nelson Mandela, Mother Theresa, Jim Collins, Bob Proctor, Mary Morrissey, and Wendy Palmer.

Because these leaders discovered, taught, and modeled **innovative ways** for being a great leader, an influential communicator, and a great human being who's creating success today and a powerful legacy for the future.

Characteristics and behaviors like empathy, taking personal responsibility, timely & effective decision making **(even in the face of risk),** and being humble... while sharing, freely giving value, leading by example, empowering others, and celebrating success.

Not only are these 7 characteristics what I've discovered... they're what I aspire to (and recommend for my clients as well): ethical & influential leadership, compassionate communication, and a way of being that **creates personal and professional success** and happiness, both today and for the long run.

• • •

How about you? Which of the 7 characteristics describe you? Where are you excelling? What can you refine?

(NOTE: This is not a place for self judgement or self recrimination. This is an opportunity for self awareness about who you are, how you do your thing, what you've created, and ways you can make things better for yourself and others.)

Being Clear on Your Purpose
Increases Your Power to Influence

Your power and ability to influence — in a bigger way — starts by being crystal clear on your purpose. This is true for individuals and it's true for companies, organizations, and movements.

When you know your purpose, these **4 things happen:**

1. Work can be more inspiring, fun, and fulfilling (since it's an expression of who you are and why you're here);

2. You get more of the right things done, faster and with less stress (since you're committed to your dream and can accept the fact that there will be hiccups, detours, and roadblocks on the way to achieving it);

3. You increase your ability to transform people's lives which is a win-win for everyone you touch (because you're able to create a much more powerful connection and resonance with others); and

4. You communicate and lead more effectively.

If you're part of a **company, organization, or movement,** purpose is just as important… because it provides meaning and a connection to the bigger picture (mission and vision). As a result, these <u>4 things happen:</u>

1. You (as well as your employees, colleagues, and/or team) are likely to be more productive, engaged, motivated, and happy;

2. There is better communication, better team spirit, & increased job satisfaction;

3. There is a greater understanding among different kinds of people which makes it easier to navigate conflict (because you're all working with a shared vision); and

4. It helps create a culture of trust and engagement while inspiring innovation.

Getting clear on your purpose is a foundation of success. But it doesn't stop there. Purpose needs to become part of the fabric of your business, organization, or movement. Like most things that are valuable in this world, it's a matter of making it happen AND making it sustainable, so you stay focused and on the right path.

So how can you do this? Rather than using values to create alignment in your business, company, organization, or movement, I invite you to **focus on principles** instead.

An Innovative Approach: Principles vs. Values

I learned something very important from Steven Covey, author of *The 7 Habits of Highly Effective People,* which changed my business.

Principles are <u>not the same as values</u>.

Here's why:

• **Values change** according to time, place, situations, and the people involved. ("A woman's place is in the home" is a powerful example. Thankfully we've come a long way from that, at least in some parts of the world.)

• **Values create your beliefs:** how you see the world, how you relate to other people, how you interpret your experiences, and how you choose to act. (And sometimes you may not even understand why you do what you do.)

• Some of your values and beliefs **may not be supporting your success**. Because values and beliefs come (unchosen) from many people, places, and situations outside of ourselves.

• Values and beliefs affect everything in your life, leadership, perspective, communication, marketing, selling, relationships, experiences, and success.

Think of it like this. Since **values are guaranteed to change,** how can you run your business (or your life) based on them?

Realistically, it's not going to work in the long run. So, I invite you to focus on principles instead.

Because **principles are like gravity.** They're a constant... expressing the core, unchanging elements of your purpose. They're like the "North Star" in your business or organization, keeping you (and everyone else) on track.

Covey's teaching (plus my own reflections) inspired me to create and implement my own 7 Principles of Influence With A Heart™.

These are based on trust, integrity, compassion, service, respect, legacy, and joy.

These 7 Principles guide my choices and decisions (big ones and little ones) in my business and in my life. They help me express my purpose by offering me inspiration, guidance, and a roadmap. Here's how they look:

1. Principle of High Integrity Success

I measure success through the people I serve, how I am living and expressing my purpose (in my life and business), and the value I create.

• Since negative thoughts, words, and actions yield negative results, I do my best to focus on the positive, even in the most challenging circumstances.

• Sometimes this requires changing my habits, beliefs, perspectives, and attitudes because they affect others, my business, and me.

2. Principle of The Other Person's Shoes

All of my choices need to be informed by more than just my own perspective. When I am about to make a choice, I remind myself to ask these questions.

• How will this choice affect my client?

• What about other people that my business touches?

• The community and the environment?

• The people who are alive, seven generations down the line from right now?

• Will everyone benefit, based on the choice that I am about to make?

3. Principle of Truth and Respect

What I think, say, and do affects me and the people around me. Because of this, I do my best to be aware of my thoughts words, and actions.

• Do I feel open, calm, and spacious… or constricted, reactive, and defensive?

• Am I telling the truth?

• Am I treating people with respect?

• How am I standing?

• What is my tone of voice?

• How can I create something beautiful and positive with what I think, say, and do?

4. Principle of Growing and Sharing Wealth

I am in business to make a difference and create wealth. The more money I make, the more people I can help.

• I know money is a result of my service and the value I bring to others, not the goal unto itself.

• Am I creating wealth responsibly, using it to serve others, and taking care of myself and my relationships… as I take this journey?

5. Principle of Community and Competition

I do my best to focus on cooperation. I know I have a far greater reach and impact by working with clients, partners, and others who, in turn, will reach out and positively affect others.

• The only competition is with myself. So I strive to grow and achieve more each day to make my business more successful, help more people, and inspire others through my ideas, message, work, and example.

6. Principle of Personal Responsibility

Because all people want to be happy, healthy, safe, and secure (just like you and me), I do my best to make choices that are aligned with my principles and are an expression of who I am… while being mindful of how these choices affect others.

• I recognize that **every person creates their reality and experiences based on habits, conditioning, history, beliefs, and attitudes.**

• Because of this, I take 100% responsibility for everything that happens to me, as well as how I affect other people.

• If something needs to change, I have the power to change it.

• I am not afraid to say, "I'm sorry."

• I also realize that other people are responsible for their own thoughts, words, choices, and actions.

7. Principle of Compassionate Service

I recognize the immense suffering in the world. At the same time, I recognize that I can help.

• Through empathy (being able to experience another person's situation by seeing the world through their eyes), I cultivate compassion which gives me the energy and inspiration to serve.

• Then I no longer focus on the suffering and problems, but shift my focus to solutions. How can I help people and the planet, through my actions today and the legacy that survives me, after I'm long gone?

These are the 7 Principles of *Influence With A Heart*. May they inspire and serve you in the best possible ways.

An Open Invitation For Us To Chat

As you know, you'll be a better leader, a more influential communicator, and make a bigger impact by using more influence… in person, online, onstage, and on the phone. This means **4 things for your business:**

1. More **people will say, "yes"** to your ideas, vision, message, products, and/or services… whether it's your clients, customers, audience, colleagues, partners, employees, stakeholders, team, and/or the media.

2. More **people will take action.** (Because more people will have the opportunity to have their business or life transformed by who you are and what you offer.)

3. **You'll be positioned** as an expert, authority, or thought leader who people know, like, and trust. (So when people invest in your training, service, product, or program — or get behind you and your vision — they will be even more invested in their success (and therefore yours).)

4. When you communicate with more influence, the people you impact will become your fans, clients, tribe, customers, community, referral network, affiliate partners, and/or more — **bringing a flood of new and repeat business to your door** — so you can make an even bigger impact!

• Think about what will happen when you inspire more people to say, "yes" — to your ideas, vision, message, products, and/or services…

• Think about what will happen when you **reach more people, cultivate more win-win relationships,** set a positive example for other businesses and leaders, and achieve more results…

• Think about what will happen when you **"turn up the volume" on your influence, income, and impact** — so you can help more people… whether it's one, or 10, or 10,000 more people…

If you want to discover how to use more influence (ethically), so you can inspire more people to say, "yes," (so it benefits them and you) contact me today.

Email ben (@) influencewithaheart.com, join my network on Linked at linkedin.com/in/bengioia, or visit InfluenceWithAHeart.com/contact to schedule a convenient time for a free consultation with me.

I look forward to speaking with you soon — and am honored to support you — as you create more influence, income, impact, and a positive legacy with your business!

Cheers,

Ben

The Framework:
Influence With A Heart™

As you know:

1. **You will be a better leader and communicator** when you use more influence;

2. Using more influence means that you use more empathy, story, and thought leadership. (By doing this, you automatically use the key principles of psychological influence... from a place of service, care, and compassion);

3. It's the same approach whether you're communicating with **one, 10, or 10,000 people** and whether you're **online, onstage, on the phone, or face-to-face.**

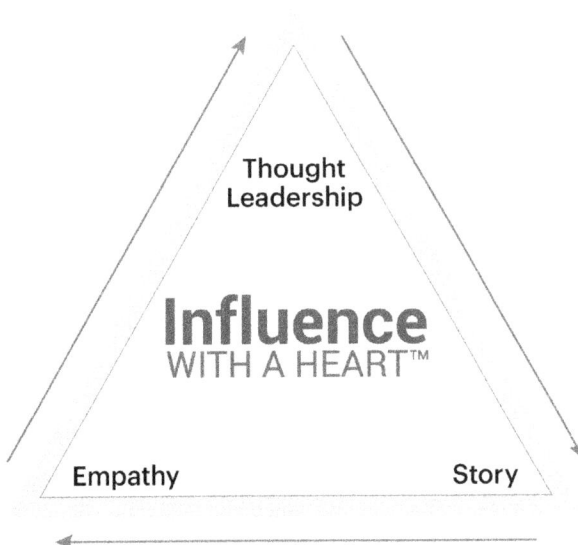

Thought
Leadership

Influence
WITH A HEART™

Empathy   Story

This Is How And Why It Works

EMPATHY

1. Empathy gives you the opportunity to see the world through another person's eyes and connect with them from a place of authenticity, integrity, and service.

2. Empathy helps you understand and have compassion for people's fears, frustrations, needs, desires, aspirations, goals, and dreams. It also helps you make better informed choices and take more effective approaches to multiple situations in your business.

3. What this means... is that **you will discover:**

• the best ways you can help your clients, customers, colleagues, and/or audience;

• what language to use for leadership, communication, and relationship marketing;

• how to give and receive feedback (skillfully);

• **what messaging, products, & services to create;** and

• how to deliver powerful, transformative value that will impact people's business or life. Or both.

4. Empathy makes people realize that you're an authentic thought leader, expert, authority, or leader who truly cares about them.

As a result, **they're inspired to tell others about you,** because they stand behind who you are, what you're about, and the impact you're creating.

STORY

1. Stories reach people's hearts as well as their minds. So your stories create inspiration… by creating an emotional experience for your reader or listener.

While logic and facts are important, **emotion is what moves people to action.** Put another way, "Facts tell, emotions sell."

2. Stories help you express your unique purpose and create a vivid vision of the future, to help your business succeed.

Stories give other people the opportunity to see the world through your eyes and stand in your shoes.

They also help to get everyone on the same page with what's being communicated.

3. Your story helps you continue to discover your unique purpose and who you are. This helps you develop more clarity, confidence, and magnetism… so more of the right people will respond to you.

4. Stories (about you, about your clients, etc.) help people know you, like you, trust you, and want to develop an ongoing relationship with you… because they allow you to **create an almost instant rapport with your audience, listener, or reader.**

THOUGHT LEADERSHIP

1. Thought leadership positions you as a reliable source of information, insight, and as a go-to person in your field or industry who is successful, can replicate success, and can teach others how to be successful, too.

2. Thought leadership shows that **you are a game changer: you're known for making a difference** in your business, organization, and/or in your world… with your inspirational ideas, innovative perspectives, and unique approach. It's your legacy, and how you keep making an impact, long after you're gone.

3. Thought leadership is how you talk about and communicate your "special sauce": your years of experience, education, failures, triumphs, anecdotes,

mishaps, insights, investment, wisdom, time, energy, effort, talent... and everything in between.

4. Thought leadership is about creating and cultivating win-win relationships, vibrant networks, and a sphere of influence that's based on trust, by connecting who you are and what you offer... to the things that people want.

In summary, **by using more empathy, story, and thought leadership** every time you're communicating or leading (which is **the simplest and most effective way** to use more influence) 3 wonderful things happen:

1. You inspire and invite people to change their thoughts — so they can choose to change their behaviors — and take action that's **good for them and good for you;**

2. You offer unique perspectives, tools, techniques, possibilities, and transformation to your clients, customers, colleagues, and/or audience; and

3. You make a bigger impact, make your business more successful, and help move the world forward.

• • •

Now that you understand the framework, let me tell you how *Influence With A Heart* started...

Ben's Story

I'd like to take just a few minutes and tell you my story, because I'd like you to know who I am, where I've been, and what I'm all about. And to let you know where my insights and discoveries have come from.

So take a moment, **take a deep breath... and imagine** me... trekking in the mountains of Southern India... with a guide named Vijay who had a really big smile.

At 6,000 feet up, it was hot, dry, and dusty... because it hadn't rained in 4 months. The sun was beating down on our heads and shoulders, and Vijay was telling me his story as we walked together along the path.

All of a sudden, from behind the trees (where I couldn't see anything), I could hear screams and shouts (not in English, of course). And then Vijay yelling, "Run!" over his shoulder as he ran off down the path.

So I ran. And ran. And ran...

I didn't know why I was running. But I knew that I was running for my life!

And this was already the second time — out of 4 times, in just 72 hours — that I almost died in India.

So as I kept running along this dry and dusty mountain path, **my life started flashing before my eyes.**

• I remembered my childhood, then high school in New York City (mostly), and then college... where I earned a BA in Psychology and a BA in Creative Writing...

• I remembered producing magazines (that were published by Hearst and Condé Nast)... and working with a variety of startups... and traveling in 16 countries...

• I remembered helping to launch *AARP The Magazine* (which was mailed to 32 million people)...

• I remembered helping two chapters of The ALS Association through an organizational consolidation, so they could support half the people in California who are living with Lou Gehrig's disease. (This was a few years before The Ice Bucket Challenge.)

• Then I remembered **that one fateful day** when I realized something that would change the entire course of my life: I was FED UP and DISCOURAGED.

• I was FED UP with the business world. Everything I could see was focused on profit... at the expense of everything and everyone else.

• I was DISCOURAGED with nonprofits because I could see that most didn't have the power, knowledge, training, or resources to make a bigger impact (even though so many nonprofits and NGOs do incredible things).

So that's when it dawned on me: ***"Hey, I want to make a bigger impact with my business... and be part of making an ongoing, major positive shift on the planet!"***

So I chose to help the individuals, companies, organizations, and movements that are already making a difference... those that want to "turn up the volume" on their influence, income, and impact.

With this clarity, I focused on becoming a top notch leader, coach, marketer, and communicator. I also started a regular meditation practice that I've been doing for more than a dozen years.

I spent years synthesizing everything I'd learned, created, and achieved: at school, in the corporate world, in the nonprofit world, and in my life. I studied with incredible coaches.

I joined masterminds with influential people and learned from powerful mentors. I studied genius copywriters. I read tons of books, took lots of courses, and took lots and lot of notes.

• The more I learned, the more action I took.

• More action meant more feedback.

• More feedback meant more clarity.

• More clarity meant (and means) more results.

I also made lots (and lots) of mistakes! So I reflected on all of these "failures," learned the lessons (some really hard ones), and cultivated my own wisdom and insights.

I was then able to take all of this knowledge plus hard-earned wisdom and use it as a strategic (and philosophical) roadmap to launch my first consulting business.

I wrote a #1 best-selling book called *Marketing With A Heart: How To Use Trust Based Marketing For Greater Income, Influence, and Impact.* I followed this with this book, called *Influence With A Heart: How To Be A Better Leader and Communicator by Using More Empathy, Story, and Thought Leadership.*

Today, **I'm grateful and blessed to speak, coach, and train** — the individuals, organizations, businesses, movements, groups, and associations — who are making a positive impact in the world.

Still Wondering How I Almost Died 4 Times?

If you're still wondering how I almost died 4 times in 72 hours in India, here's what happened:

#1 was when my bus completely demolished a guardrail and almost went over the edge, as it skidded around the tight curve of windy mountain road…

#2 was when my guide Vijay and me — were running and running and running from an out-of-control, blazing forest fire — that was going to destroy the nearby village (and us) if we didn't get away as quickly as possible…

#3 was when we stumbled upon a snake — small, green, and deadly — on the path in front of us…

(Thank goodness for Vijay… because I didn't see it!)

#4 was encountering a mountain lion (that somehow, miraculously, ran off)…

That entire, terrifying, eye-opening, nerve wracking experience was perhaps **the best 72 hours of my life.** Because it gave me a gift… an overflowing gratitude for life… and a fire inside to create massive positive impact.

That's why you and I are both here today. So let's dig in!

Chapter 1:
EMPATHY

Thought
Leadership

Influence
WITH A HEART™

Empathy   Story

Summary: EMPATHY

1. Empathy gives you the opportunity to see the world through another person's eyes and connect with them from a place of authenticity, integrity, and service.

2. Empathy helps you understand and have compassion for people's fears, frustrations, needs, desires, aspirations, goals, and dreams. It also helps you make better informed choices and take more effective approaches to multiple situations in your business.

3. **What this means...** is that you will discover:

• the best ways you can help your clients, customers, colleagues, and/or audience;
• what language to use for leadership, communication, and marketing;
• how to give and receive feedback (skillfully);
• what messaging, products, & services to create; and
• how to deliver powerful, transformative value that will impact people's business or life. Or both.

4. Empathy makes people realize that you're an authentic **thought leader, expert, authority, or leader** who truly cares about them. As a result, they're inspired to tell others about you, because they stand behind who you are, what you're about, and the impact you're creating.

Influence Is About Shaping The Future, So Connect The Dots and Make Your Vision Clear

Whether you're an executive, entrepreneur, speaker, author, coach, trainer, consultant, or other visionary — who's committed to making a positive change in the world — you are a leader.

You're a leader because you are shaping the future, as well as your own reality. You're bringing your vision, story, message, idea, product, or service to the world.

Because of this, it's critical to communicate with people in a way that educates and inspires them to take action.

You must **connect the dots from your vision to their goals and dreams.** Don't assume they'll get it. Make the path clear.

(This is because you're competing with so much noise and distraction, that we all face, every day.)

Do this with your prospects, customers, clients, vendors, partners, managers, stockholders, co-workers, employees, government, media, communities, and/or your board of directors.

Everyone your business touches.

Apparently, there are lots of different groups here… with an astounding array of goals, challenges, fears, pains, hopes, desires, and dreams. Keep connecting the dots. **Important:** you can't talk to all of these people — about the same things — or use the same language.

1. Instead, begin with empathy: get to know your audience and speak to them, in their language, about the things that are most important to them.

2. **Ask people to share their stories with you,** so you can understand even more of what's going on for them. Ask questions. Ask more questions. Go deep.

3. **Tell people your story,** so they have the chance to know, like, and trust you, while seeing you as the expert, thought leader, authority, or leader that you truly are.

When you take these 3 steps, the magic happens:

You understand them, they understand you, and you have everything you need for visionary leadership, effective relationship marketing, communication, and authentic human connection… that can create real transformation.

When you use more empathy, you can inspire people to make the choices that will benefit them, benefit you, and benefit the world.

Using The Psychology of Influence (Ethically)

An amazing resource about the psychology of influence is a book called *Influence,* by Robert Cialdini. You'll understand how and why people say, "yes" — and then how to use these insights (ethically) in your business. You'll learn the 6 principles of influence: <u>knowing, liking, trust, authority, reciprocity, and consistency</u>.

You want to be sure use these every time you're communicating. So people will know you, like you, trust you, and see you as an expert or authority. Then they will invest in your products or services, get behind you and your vision, and give you the opportunity to serve them.

Even before you start reading Cialdini's book, always remember this: there are **3 things that motivate people.**

1. They want to achieve happiness and avoid suffering.

2. They want to overcome their internal struggles of self-doubt, fear, worry, anxiety, and/or insecurity.

3. They're searching for greater meaning, purpose, and connection in a rapidly changing world that's in a vast and mysterious universe.

So start using more empathy, today, and you'll be able to authentically connect with people around these 3 things.

How Well Do You Know Who You're Talking To?

If you want to connect and develop a trusting relationship with your prospect, customer, client, colleague, and/or audience… you'll want to communicate in their language about the things that are the most important to them.

This means using the <u>exact words and phrases</u> that they're saying (or writing) when they describe their challenges, fears, frustrations, needs, experiences, hopes, goals, desires, and dreams.

Around the world, we speak different languages, practice different customs, and do different things.

This is a reality: country to country, business to business, culture to culture, generation to generation, situation to situation, and person to person.

So it's critical to get super clear on what's important to people — and **how *they* talk about it** — so you can create the most effective communication, rapport, connection.

To get started, do your research, talk to lots of people, and make sure you're as clear as possible with these 3 things:

1. **Key Data** (Demographics) that can be measured, like gender, age, income, marital status, etc. — the "dry," (perhaps) and vitally important facts about your clients, customers, employees, team, market, or audience.

2. **Group Trends** (Psychographics) such as behaviors, hobbies, spending habits, values/principles, product usage, opinions, where they hang out online, interests, and lifestyle choices.

3. **Individual Purpose and Passion** (Sociographics) which goes deep, giving you an understanding of what motivates people: their personal needs, attitudes, fears, frustrations, goals, dreams, and what gives meaning to their lives.

These allow you to connect with people on an emotional and experiential level, which is what you want. Then you can use the right language for better marketing, more influential communication, creating tailored products/ services, and leadership that creates transformation.

Again, remember those 3 things that motivate people:

1. They want to achieve happiness and avoid suffering.

2. They want to overcome their internal struggles of self-doubt, fear, worry, anxiety, and/or insecurity.

3. They're searching for greater meaning, purpose, and connection in a rapidly changing world that's in a vast and mysterious universe.

Knowing as much of this information as possible will help you **expand your sphere of influence** as you *discover other people* who are connected to your client/customer.

This gives you the opportunity to serve a wider range of people, businesses, and/or organizations.

Here's how to uncover this information *(in no specific order):*

1. Ask questions.

2. Do your research.

3. Email people.

4. Make calls.

5. Give a talk.

6. Offer a webinar.

7. Start or participate in a LinkedIn group, mastermind group, or in-person networking group.

The more that you know about your client/customer/audience/colleague/market — from their day-to-day experiences to the deep, emotional details — the more successful you will be.

• You'll **connect, communicate, and lead better.**

• You'll reach more people with your ideas and message.

• You'll create a shared human connection and experience while getting people excited about who you are, what you're about, and how you're going to make a positive impact in their business or life.

Or both.

• You'll **create superior products and services that deliver exceptional value** (based on what they want and need, because they've told you).

• You'll be able to discover even more people like them to serve (since you've clearly articulated who you help and how you help them).

• You'll **energize even more people** with your vivid vision of the future, and show them a way to get there.

And the people you inspire will tell others about you!

Elevating Your Elevator Pitch

Very often, opportunity starts with the question,
"So, what do you do?"

Very often, you only have a few seconds to get — and then hold — a person's attention as you're answering.

So how do you do it? How do you hold this person's attention... AND give him or her the answer that clearly and effectively communicates the best and right combination of:

1) who you help & how you help them;

2) who you are & why you care about what you do; and

3) a dash of your **"special sauce"**... so they remember you?

Hint: people may forget what you say and do, but they'll never forget the way they feel, thanks to you. (Inspired by the poet Maya Angelou.)

The first thing to do is start right there. **Connect with their emotions.** Think of affecting the ways that people feel (ethically, of course). Talk about the things might be on their mind.

Instead of focusing on yourself and what you want, focus on this other person: what they want/need and their experience (their struggle, dream, or both).

From there, remember, **this not a pitch... it's a cascade.**

(That's why I call it an "elevated" elevator pitch.)

Sadly, most people still think it's a pitch. And they treat it like a pitch. A one shot deal. The big "at bat." A home run... or nothing.

But they couldn't be farther from the truth.

Because **every "yes" is made up of series of "yeses."** And building interest (just like cultivating relationships) operates much the same way. Think of dominoes.

Or a waterfall.

You'll notice that the water doesn't fall directly from the top to the bottom. The water cascades — from level to level, step to step — top to bottom. (Another analogy: on your first date, you don't ask your date to marry you.)

So (before) the next time you're asked, *"What do you do?",* consider your response...

What will you say — and in what sequence — so that:

1. this person will get to know, like, and trust you;

2. you position yourself as a caring expert, leader, authority, or thought leader;

3. you connect the dots — from what they want and need — to who you are and what you offer; and

4. you keep sparking interest, so the person you're speaking with keeps asking you, "Tell me more…?"

If you're not sure, simply **go back to basics:** people want to be seen, heard, and understood. The want to overcome their challenges and achieve their dreams. And for all this to happen, these people MUST know, like, and trust you.

(This has been going on since the beginning of time.)

So ask them to share a story (of themselves, an experience, a case study, a success, a challenge, etc.)

And then share a story, about you, with them.

When you do this, **you create the cascade that gives this person an opportunity** to have their business and/or life impacted by who you are and what you offer.

[What Are You Thoughts or Insights?]

Case Study: Purpose Is The Foundation

OPPORTUNITY I delivered a 2-day training for a global organization at Stanford University. The audience (126 leaders) learned how to improve communication and team engagement. The day began with getting clear on purpose: as individuals, then connecting their's to the organization's.

BACKGROUND When people understand their purpose and how that fits into the larger purpose of their company or organization, communication and leadership are more effective. People are often more productive, engaged, motivated, and happy.

SOLUTION I worked with the audience so they could get clear about purpose. By using empathy and story, they learned innovative approaches to leadership and team building. The training also included mindfulness, a bit of neuroscience, and nonverbal communication approaches.

RESULTS *"An amazing two days! I learned so much from you and loved your teaching!"*
  "Your training and coaching are highly effective and extremely practical. I will definitely use my new skills!"
  "You taught us how new ways to communicate with our team (and with my wife as well)... I think that's great!"
  "We can use this method to build better relationships with our colleagues AND employees."

ACTION: Use More Empathy In All of Your Communication With These 5 Simple Steps

1. **Imagine** that the person you're communicating with is your best friend... and someone who wants to be happy, safe, healthy, and free (just like you);

2. **Imagine** having a heart-to-heart discussion... about their dreams and challenges... what keeps them up at night... what they can't get out of their heads... what they want and need... and what they want to achieve in their business and in their life;

3. **Empathize** with them, acknowledge them, and let them know that they are not alone; that it is okay, there is hope, and that you are the one who can help them (or you will teach them how to help themselves);

4. **Show** them how to get past their pain or challenge starting today, and over the long haul... then teach them how to reach their dreams as quickly and effectively as possible (in a way that supports who they are);

5. (Based on your "discussion") **capture** this information:

• What words were they using?
• What information were they sharing with you?
• What emotions were coming up (for them and you)?

- How were they describing their experience?
- What stories were they telling?

Now that you have these answers, use them (ethically) in all of your communications, starting today. <u>Because 5 amazing things are going to happen:</u>

First, you'll discover what's really going on in people's lives, what they're experiencing, what's motivating them (fears to dreams), and how you can best serve them.

Second, you'll have the language you need to speak (and write) to them. By using the exact words they're using, you'll connect, deeply and authentically, with them.

Third, you'll automatically be positioned as the person who can help them. *(Why? Because when you can articulate someone's pain, challenge, or dream in their own words — or even better than they would describe it — people often assume that you have the solution... or that you can help them find it for themselves.)*

Fourth, you'll know what products, services, or strategies to offer... and how to position, package, and present them in a way that offers extreme value.

Fifth, it will help you create a community, tribe, or following of people who are committed to your vision.

Chapter 2:
STORY

Thought
Leadership

Influence
WITH A HEART™

Empathy   Story

Page 71

Summary: STORY

1. Stories reach people's hearts as well as their minds. So **your stories create inspiration...** by creating an emotional experience for your reader or listener.

While logic and facts are important, emotion is what moves people to action. Put another way, "Facts tell, emotions sell."

2. Stories help you express your unique purpose and create a vivid vision of the future, to help your business succeed. Stories give other people the opportunity to see the world through your eyes and stand in your shoes.

They also help to get everyone on the same page with what's being communicated.

3. Your story helps you continue to **discover your unique purpose** and who you are. This helps you develop more clarity, confidence, and magnetism... so more of the right people will respond to you.

4. Stories (about you, about your clients, etc.) help people know you, like you, trust you, and want to develop an ongoing relationship with you... because they allow you to create an almost instant rapport with your audience, listener, or reader.

The Power of Story In Leadership

More than any other time in history, our society and our businesses need leaders, the kind of leaders that care about the good of humanity and the planet.

You're a leader, whether you call yourself that or not. You're a leader, whether you're helping one person or changing the lives of millions.

Because real leadership isn't about titles. It's about caring for the people you serve and creating new realities in business, in your life, and in the world.

If you ask most high performers, self-development experts, brain scientists, and spiritual teachers, one of the fastest and most effective ways to create new realities (for yourself and others) is through stories.

Sharing your story — and discovering other people's stories — are key components of marketing to, communicating with, and/or leading a diverse array of people. (Essentially, you're creating new realities.) This can include any/all of the following:

1. your prospects, customers, clients, audience…

2. your employees, vendors, partners…

3. managers, stockholders, co-workers, colleagues...

4. the government, the media, your local community, and your board of directors...

5. Basically, anyone (and everyone) that your business impacts.

When you share your story, people will take an extra moment to read your words or hear what you say.

When you listen to their stories... these same people will realize that you understand and care about them.

• Stories make ideas and concepts tangible... while making books fun to read, podcasts fun to listen to in the car, and speeches fun to hear.

• Stories are what helps make the learning stick... so the things that you discover become part of your "muscle memory"... so they're available to use again and again.

• Stories help you move your clients, customers, colleagues, or audience from inspiration... to action... to satisfaction.

• (You'll have an audience that will be hanging onto your every word... whether it's 1 or 10 or 10,000 people.)

Stories don't have to take hours and hours. You can tell a story in an instant, with a gesture, or with a smile. You can tell a story with an image, a handful of words, or a tweet. You can tell a story through video, email, or any medium that connects you to the people who are important to your business.

This is so important… whether you're teaching, coaching, selling, serving, training, speaking, or leading.

Because you're inspiring people and connecting the dots… from your vision, to their goals and dreams. You're **educating and influencing your audience to take action,** so it benefits them and benefits you.

That's the power of story.

7 Things Happen When You Use Story

1. Stories will help get people to your website, onto your list, calling you for a consultation, investing in your products and services — and telling the world about what you offer — because it's changing their business or their life for the better.

2. Using more story (which includes your signature story, case studies, client success profiles, testimonials, and even what you learned while riding the bus yesterday) will

Page 75

help make your business more profitable… so you can make a bigger impact. People will remember you because of the stories that you share.

3. You'll be influencing people to take action by appealing to reason… and emotion. **(This is what you want.)**

4. When you discover and listen to someone else's story, you create the ongoing opportunity for them to know, like, trust, and see you as an expert, authority, or thought leader.

5. When you share your stories, people will understand you AND your vision. They will be inspired to follow your lead.

6. Although this is a world of different languages, cultures, and businesses, stories help people realize that we have much more in common than we have differences.

7. You'll be able to impact more lives every single day.

There isn't a **social change, movement, or paradigm shift** that's ever happened… without stories. When there are no stories, no one listens.

But when you share your stories, people can't stop listening to you!

Your Story Is Your "Special Sauce"

Your story is an important part of who you are. Stories are the articulation of vision. Your story is **your "special sauce":** your years of experience, education, failures, triumphs, anecdotes, mishaps, insights, investment, wisdom, time, energy, effort, talent… and everything in between.

Your stories can include any and all of the following:

1. your signature story, "mess-to-success" moments, detours, and successes;

2. case studies and testimonials;

3. anecdotes about your colleagues/customer/clients and/or audience;

4. their successes, challenges, goals, and dreams;

5. their experience of you or your company… via your vision, idea, message, product, or service;

6. relevant bits of the news/science/history/literature/ popular culture/an interesting that happened to you last week, etc.;

7. your purpose, guiding principles, and how you help make transformation and results happen.

You have important stories. **Your stories are key** to what YOU offer to the world and the results that YOU bring to people's businesses and lives. That's valuable stuff.

When you share your story, people will take an extra moment to read your words or hear what you're saying.

Because stories make concepts and ideas real and tangible… since they connect with people on an emotional level. I'll say it again: stories reach people's hearts as well as their minds.

Stories connect the dots between the perceptual and conceptual parts of your experience. And they make what you're saying so much more interesting!

It's one thing to hear or read the word "fruit."

It's a completely different experience when you hear about, or read, or see an image… of a juicy red apple, in the hands of a smiling child who's getting ready to take (another) big bite… as the juice is already running down her chin…

That's the power of story.

Stories are key: whether you're teaching, coaching, selling, serving, training, speaking, or leading. Because your story will help you connect the dots… from your vision to people's goals and dreams.

Stories create opportunities for people to get to know you… while positioning you as the leader, expert, authority, or thought leader that you are.

• This means that people will like you, trust you, and understand that you care about them and their experience.

• They'll realize that you truly see who they are, what they're facing, and what they want to achieve most.

• They'll know that you're the person who can help them get there… and be delighted to say, "yes" to you.

In essence, stories are one of the best ways to use Cialdini's 6 **Principles of Influence.**

When you share stories, **here's what happens:**

1. You'll be establishing the connection from a person's head to their heart.

2. You'll be inspiring them to take action that's good for them and good for you.

3. You'll have an audience that will be hanging onto your every word. Whether it's one or 10 or 10,000 people.

(That's why stories are good for your business.)

I always use stories in my teaching, coaching, writing, training, and speeches. Because — in a world with a dazzling array of cultures, customs, countries, language, dialects, geography, history, and politics — **stories are the most direct method to bridge the gaps among different people.**

• You can tell a story with an image or a picture, a handful of words, or even a 140 character #Tweet.

• You can tell a story through video, email, or any communication medium that connects you to the people you serve.

• You can tell a story in an instant, with a gesture, or with your smile.

Stories give us the chance to speak from the heart and connect with the hearts of the people near us, across the country, and around the world.

Logic (Alone) Never Changed The World

One of the most important things I learned about being a better leader and communicator is this: how to mindfully choose how you respond to people, circumstances, events, and your own thoughts.

This all started in South Africa in 2002 and then continued in 2003, when I spent a few of months traveling around, then living in Cape Town.

While I was there, I learned two things **(thanks to Nelson Mandela)** that inspired a transformation in my business and completely shifted my life.

The first thing I learned from Mandela (affectionately known as "Madiba") was about freedom.

It came from his example: how he responded to being locked up for 27 years in a South African prison, during apartheid.

All that time, he strove to keep his vision (his story) for a free South Africa alive.

The lesson: **no matter what happens, you can choose to respond instead of reacting.**

Think about it. The ways that people treat you is an *outward expression of how they treat themselves*. It has nothing to do with your value as a person.

That's a powerful truth.

And when you keep this truth on your radar, you immediately empower yourself.

You're more able to make a choice… from moment to moment… to respond, rather than react.

Basically, you're influencing your own capability (and therefore yourself) to make more powerful choices, more often.

For Madiba, this wasn't always easy. In fact, it was probably never easy.

But he kept at it, because he knew that freedom starts on the inside.

He knew, just like we all know, that we're chock full of knee-jerk reactions… just waiting to be unleashed.

Big ones, little ones, and everything-in-between ones.

But, in those beautiful moments…

… when you are able to choose…

… to make a conscious choice and *respond*…

… **you are literally creating freedom** inside of yourself!

Freedom from these 4 things:

1. Reaction (even if only for a moment).

2. Habit (the ones that no longer serve you).

3. The past.

4. The future.

Freedom is right now — in this one beautiful moment — a moment that's filled with all the seeds of possibility for something new, something different, something better for the world, and for yourself.

Something better, for Mandela.

27 years in prison under the apartheid regime… then he was elected President in 1994.

What an incredible journey, transformation, and example of unparalleled leadership!

And The Story Continues...

If you take even a few minutes to learn more about Madiba, you'll see something amazing.

• *One person who gave himself permission — to discover the gifts of an incredibly dark situation — so he could influence his own life and the course of an entire country.*

And this leads us to the second thing I learned from Madiba. It's also about freedom.

This time, it's freedom that comes from forgiveness.

What happened under apartheid in South Africa resulted in violence and human rights abuses from all sides. No part of society escaped this.

South Africa took a revolutionary approach to healing: truth, reconciliation, and the possibility of forgiveness on a large scale (through their Truth and Reconciliation Commission).

In a nutshell, the TRC offered public hearings where victims/survivors could share stories and possibly confront former abusers (creating an opportunity for forgiveness and greater societal healing).

This powerful action (on a national level) showed me that it is possible to bring forgiveness into a larger arena.

Because when you start forgiving others, you create more freedom for yourself.

• *More forgiveness = more freedom.*

• *More freedom = more power.*

• *More power = more influence.*

More influence means that you and I can do even more great things in the world, and make a bigger impact, whether it's helping one or 10 or 10,000 more people.

Because this road to freedom is a long one:

1. In our hearts;

2. In our minds; and

3. In the world around us.

Remember, it's a marathon, not a sprint. And the only way we will get there, is together.

So let's create a legacy that takes all of us there.

[What Are You Thoughts or Insights?]

.

Page 86

Case Study: Pivoting and Positioning

OPPORTUNITY A boutique tech company wanted to attract more businesses with positive social impact. The founder also wanted more time to volunteer, by teaching.

BACKGROUND The company was known for an app that helps California wine growers reduce water usage and costs. They created technology for a healthcare system to improve services for people with AIDS (50 states).

SOLUTION Through collaborative exploration, interviews, and capturing stories, I guided the founder in identifying and clarifying the new positioning which created two client pipelines: 1) leaders/decision makers; and 2) developers. Although two different markets, they wanted the same outcomes. They just spoke about them differently. As a result, we adapted marketing and communications to effectively accommodate these insights while presenting the founder as a thought leader.

We transformed his entire website, LinkedIn summary & tagline, social media descriptions, elevator pitch, optin content, email sequence, discovery call script, and began developing a product.

RESULTS New business is already coming in via both pipelines and the founder has just been asked to teach at a big tech event in San Francisco.

ACTION: Choose 13 of Your Best Stories By Using These 7 Guidelines

As you learned, **"story" and "stories" can mean:**

1. your signature story, "mess-to-success" moments, detours, and successes;

2. case studies and testimonials;

3. anecdotes about your colleagues/customer/clients and/or audience;

4. their successes, challenges, goals, and dreams;

5. their experience of you or your company... via your vision, idea, message, product, or service;

6. relevant bits of the news/science/history/literature/ popular culture/an interesting that happened to you last week, etc.;

7. your purpose, guiding principles, and how you help make transformation and results happen.

So, how do you choose which stories to capture, clarify, and communicate? Remember that it all comes back to using more influence. You want to choose the stories that:

1. Inspire people to change their ideas, change their minds, and make things happen; and

2. Are brimming with Cialdini's Principles of Influence.

So your stories need to paint the pictures — that give your audience the opportunity to know, like, and trust you — while seeing you as an expert or an authority who's in it for the "win-win."

Here's how:

1. Choose 3 stories about yourself that clearly indicate you are a reliable source of information and a go-to person in your field.

2. Come up with 5 brief anecdotes or illustrations that connect the dots from who you are and what you offer... to the outcomes that people want.

3. Think of all your unique stories. What can you share that expresses YOU, the unique and wonderful YOU?

4. Capture a story that helped inspire your purpose or speaks to the beautiful heart that you have.

5. Select your 3 biggest professional successes and write about them (in a way that shows tangible outcomes).

6. As you articulate any of these stories, draw upon other aspects of your life whether personal, professional, or anything in between (without compromising your privacy, of course).

7. In creative writing classes, the professors teach, "Show, don't tell." For our purposes, we want to, "Show AND Tell."

So this means:

A. YES! Paint the pictures…

B. Make your stories multisensory (use as many of the 5 senses (plus emotion) as you are able); and

C. Tell your reader, audience, or listener (in no uncertain terms) about the picture you just painted for them.

D. Speak, write, and connect from the heart as well as the mind. **To do this, simply become aware** of (or put your hand over) your heart (for just a moment) as you speak, write, connect, train, or teach.

E. Keep a file of these stories available and accessible.

Chapter 3:

THOUGHT LEADERSHIP

Summary: THOUGHT LEADERSHIP

1. Thought leadership positions you as a reliable source of information, insight, and as a go-to person in your field or industry who is **successful, can replicate success, and can teach others how** to be successful, too.

2. Thought leadership shows that you are a game changer: you're known for making a difference in your business, organization, and/or in your world… with your **inspirational ideas, innovative perspectives, and unique approach.** It's your legacy, and how you keep making an impact, long after you're gone.

3. Thought leadership is how you talk about and communicate your "special sauce": your years of experience, education, failures, triumphs, anecdotes, mishaps, insights, investment, wisdom, time, energy, effort, talent… and everything in between.

4. Thought leadership is about creating and cultivating win-win relationships, vibrant networks, and a sphere of influence that's based on trust, by connecting who you are and what you offer… to the outcomes that people want.

Thought Leadership Is Influence In Action and A Key Component of Your Story

Thought leadership is an interesting term. Lots of people use it. Lots of people claim that they are "thought leaders." Lots of people define it in lots of different ways.

For me — thought leadership is **influence in action** — **and a key component of your story.**

I was recently having a conversation with a new client, and she said something very interesting:

"I find that I have internal resistance to the idea of being a 'thought leader.' Somehow I've created an image in my head of what 'real' thought leaders look like, and so I struggle with the notion of including myself in that group… "

The first thing I said (gently, and with so much love) was, *"Get over it."* (We both laughed.)

Then I said, *"Ok, it's time to own your thought leadership (and your power) for these 7 reasons":*

1. *"… it's taking what you know, who you serve (and why), and your "special sauce" — and expressing that to your audience — whether you're online, onstage, on*

the phone, or in person. Because you know it will help people with their business and in their life.

2. *"Your thought leadership is uniquely yours because it's based on your years of experience, education, failures, triumphs, insights, investment, wisdom, time, energy, effort, talents… and everything in between.*

3. *"Thought leadership is the part of your story that articulates your expertise, authority, capability, and leadership.* **People want to know these things about you.**

4. *"It will help you create a community, tribe, or following of people who are committed to your vision… because* **they trust you and you're helping them** *to realize their goals and achieve their dreams.*

5. *"It's an important part of inspiring people to take action, because you're offering them new insights and perspectives… while providing an evolving roadmap for success.*

6. *"These inspired* **people will literally become the voice of your company or organization…** *and the ones who bring a flood of new and repeat business to your door.*

7. *"It will help you create and cultivate powerful relationships so you can move new ideas and possibilities*

from person to person, throughout organizations, and throughout the world, and into the future."

Do you consider yourself a thought leader?

If you're not sure, then I invite you to take this **40-second quiz:**

1. Am I a reliable source of information and a go-to person in my field of expertise?

2. Do I inspire people with innovative ideas?

3. Do I create relationships based on trust?

4. Do I turn my ideas into success, and can I show others how to replicate that success?

5. Am I known for making a difference in one person's life? Several lives? In my organization? In my world?

Now... based on your answers, are you a thought leader? (I would guess yes!)

Yes, you are a thought leader.

So if you want to be perceived as one, simply use more thought leadership every time you communicate.

How To Position Yourself As A Leader In Your Field or Industry

Think of your <u>positioning</u> as the articulation and presentation of:

• **Who you are** (professionally… a likable and trustworthy, leader, expert, thought leader, or authority);

• **What you offer** (and why it's unique to you); and

• **How this connects** (with what people want).

Based on these, here are 10 things that are critical for you to keep making people aware of:

1. Your unique perspective/framework/approach;

2. How well you synthesize and deliver information so it's manageable, accessible, understandable, and offers a new insight or twist;

3. How consistent you are in your communications (for top of mind awareness);

4. How many places you can be found in the marketplace;

5. How many raving fans you have (not just browsers);

6. How current your brand feels;

7. What level of clientele you work with (based on your level of expertise at the current time... (while holding the intention to take it to the next level, of course));

8. How long you have been serving;

9. Your energy and passion (as others experience it); and

10. The stories you tell about yourself and other people.

By integrating these 10 components into your regular communication — **you'll automatically be positioned as the person who has the answer or solution** that your clients, customers, colleagues or audience are looking for — or the message, product, or service that will help them discover the answers and solutions for themselves.

Think of it like this, by considering these two images:

1. "You're standing in the river."

If you want to catch more fish, you'll be more successful if you're standing in the river with a net than if you're standing on the shore and yelling, "Hey, fish, come over here... I have what you want!"

• *Said another way, it's almost impossible to influence people to click, follow, read, buy, and/or invest in what you offer… if you position yourself in and around something that nobody wants and they're not looking for (even if you know they need it).*

2. "You're standing in the river, away from the crowd."

While you want to be where the fish are, you don't want to stand in the part of the river where everyone else is fishing (because it's too crowded).

• *Said another way, the goal of your positioning is to express who you are — through your business — in a unique way,* **so you can stand out in the marketplace or in your niche.** *Then, people will be attracted to you, because they need what you offer and they realize you're the right person (or company) to serve them.*

EXAMPLE. When I launched my businesses, and wrote my books (*Marketing With A Heart* and then *Influence With A Heart*), I recognized the need for quality leadership, influential communication, and marketing.

To begin, I recognized that people in every industry are always looking for expert, trustworthy help that delivers real outcomes. **("I'm standing in the river.")**

At the same time, I was able to differentiate myself and create success by adding the "With A Heart" component. **("I'm standing in the river, away from the crowd.")**

Because these days, most people don't want:

• old school, sleazy "used-car-salesman" marketing;
• communication that lacks empathy and connection; and
• command-and-control leadership;

They want leadership, communication, and marketing that's ethical, delivers exceptional value, and aligns with their principles of integrity, trust, respect, value, and service.

That's why people kept hiring me for speaking, coaching, and consulting. **It gave me more reach, I got a better response, and therefore I was able to produce more results** (for my clients and myself). And I'm happy and grateful to report that this keeps happening.   :)

• • •

(Thanks to Brendon Burchard for the inspiration for this piece. I love how he teaches about the importance of unique positioning and how it applies to the success of your business and your ability to make a bigger impact.)

One of The Biggest Mistakes Thought Leaders Make When Communicating

My friend Jorge is a dynamic and dynamite speaker and leader.

The first time I saw him, I was riveted. He delivered the perfect combination of information, inspiration, and stories that made his teaching come alive… and influenced a powerful perspective shift in his audience.

But when I saw how he writes… uh oh.

Have you ever noticed how some smart, influential people don't always write the way they speak?

That's Jorge.

When he speaks to an audience — or one-to-one — he's flawless.

His written words, however, are kind of flawed.

And this is a big problem because people aren't subscribing to his email list. (Jorge wants to build his list so he can attract more business and not rely solely on speaking gigs, networking, and referrals.)

So he and I spent some time looking at his website, emails, blog posts, and the language (and incentive) he's using to invite people to join his list.

I analyzed what he wrote... with an understanding of what he was trying to accomplish.

His 7 biggest mistakes (which are common for many consultants, leaders, experts, authors, and thought leaders) were these:

1. **Too many words** and too many big words;

2. **Too many ideas**, at once, that are too complex and abstract;

3. **Too many tangents,** sidebars, and open loops;

4. **Too many long sentences** with too many commas;

5. **Too little focus** on what the client (customer, and/or audience) really needs (not what you think they need);

6. **Too little focus** on this person's (or group's) fears, frustrations, challenges, aspirations, goals, and/or dreams — described from their perspective and experience — in their language; and

7. **Too little focus** on "connecting the dots." (What kind of transformation are you offering? Why is this so important in this person's business and/or life? Why are you uniquely suited to serve this person — or these people — more than anyone else out there?)

The results?

1. Fewer people read. Not so many take action. Hardly anyone invests.

2. Less reach, response, and results (lots of wasted time, money, and energy). <u>Less impact.</u>

So I offered a solution that Jorge was able to implement right away: record what you say into dictation software or get it transcribed.

<u>Here's why it works</u>:

Just like Jorge, when you create any kind of content… whether it's an email, blog post, training, speech, video, book, Facebook post, webinar, information product… basically anything… you'll want to communicate with people in YOUR VOICE.

Not your academic or business voice. **YOUR VOICE.**

The voice that speaks your truth and explains who you are, what you do, why you do it… and shows people that you can help them overcome their challenges and reach their goals dreams.

Since the words from Jorge's mouth are clearly hitting their mark… all he needs to do is get them down on paper, so to speak.

Then he can **USE HIS OWN WORDS** (the ones that are inspiring and influential) to write his emails, update his website, refine his LinkedIn summary, and make his opt-in content even better and even more valuable.

So, here's how Jorge did it, and how you can do it too:

Create an outline (as you would for a speech, presentation, article, blog post, webinar, or training) that describes these 4 things:

1. Who you are, what you do, and why you're uniquely suited to do it… like nobody else on the planet.

2. The transformation you help people create — at home, at work, or in their lives — and connect this to your story.

(You'll be extra influential if you share how you discovered your knowledge and earned your wisdom.)

3. The 1-3-5 steps/ways/methods a person can begin that transformation, starting today.

4. The best next action for this person to take.

Then talk your way through the outline in your own voice (whether you're dictating or getting it transcribed).

Because when you communicate with people in "your voice," you're able to accomplish <u>4 things</u>:

1. **You connect deeply, clearly, and on an emotional (as well as expert) level...** whether it's with your prospects, customers, clients, colleagues, and/or anyone that's important for your business)...

2. **You create rapport...** so you can give people the opportunity to know you, like you, trust you, and see that you are a credible authority or leader;

3. **You deliver valuable information...** that makes a powerful transformation in their business or their life;

4. **You invite them to take action...** that's good for them and good for you.

So, that being said, are you ready to record?

7 Reasons Why The Buddha Was
(and Still Is) An Influential Thought Leader

For more than 40 years, the Buddha served people by teaching a nonsectarian way to live a more harmonious life… where happiness comes from the inside and doesn't depend on what's happening outside of us.

He discovered a practice that worked for him, worked for other people, *and* could be taught. His message, teaching, and how he delivered them — have created an ongoing legacy — and make him one of the most influential thought leaders in human history.

Here are 7 reasons why:

1. The Buddha tailored his vision, message, and teaching to his audience. No matter who he was talking to — woman or man, queen, king, or peasant — he always **spoke to people in a language that they understood.** He met them where they were, not where they "should" be.

2. He used story and analogy to clarify his point, to provide a learning experience that was much more holistic than straight theory, and much more memorable over time. He taught in a way was accessible, was applicable in daily life, and gave immediate as well as long-term benefits and results.

3. The Buddha always invited people to try his system out… to **verify the results for themselves,** and not just accept them on blind faith.

4. He presented his teachings simply and directly: as frameworks, steps, and a clear process. He made sure that his teaching was available to everyone who wanted to listen and practice.

5. He created an aligned mission, vision, principles, method, and message that became his brand. This created a growing community that practiced the teachings and spread them to others.

6. The Buddha taught that **the only constant, is change.** Because of that, each of us has an opportunity every single moment to change: what we think, say, and do — so we can break free from the places we're stuck — and live happier, more peaceful, more successful lives.

7. He knew that the only way to keep the teachings intact and available for generations to come, was to deliver them in a variety of ways: different methods, diverse perspectives, various analogies, and multiple angles. (Yet, always following the same core, guiding principles.)

I'd say it worked! His teachings have been around for almost 2,600 years and are practiced all over the world.

[What Are You Thoughts or Insights?]

Page 107

Case Study: Using Business For Good

OPPORTUNITY A San Francisco nonprofit (a local Chapter of a national organization) needed help during Phase 2 of its launch. The company helps bring proven profitable, conscious business practices to organizations and leaders (Bay Area and Silicon Valley).

BACKGROUND The company was facing a challenge: how to quickly and effectively scale their membership and sponsorship numbers and put themselves "on the map" in the conscious business space... in a way that makes them unique AND positions them to complement other like-minded organizations (products and services).

SOLUTION By working directly with the board, I created a relationship marketing and communications strategy that helped position the organization as a thought leader. We identified the right partnering opportunities, new ways of delivering value, and building networks. Through live events (with a range of topics, taught by an array of experts), we built a loyal, diverse community.

RESULTS The strategies and system for both communications and marketing increased membership by 37% and sponsorship by 30%, created the revenue stream to begin hiring staff, and positively influenced the strategic actions of the national, parent organization.

ACTION: Are You A Thought Leader? (Make Sure People Know These 7 Things About You)

1. Your position, title, job, role, company, etc....

2. Your professional path (your successes, case studies, etc.) as well as your earned wisdom from your "failures").

3. The fact that you do a lot of good for a lot of people already... as indicated by your many testimonials.

4. Anytime that you appear in the media or press, as seen on, as quoted in, as featured in, etc.

5. Your partnerships and connections to influencers.

6. Your philosophy, framework, "special sauce," etc.

7. Your book, awards, testimonials, accolades, products, inventions, innovations, etc.

People's perception of you as a thought leader is key for your success and ability to make a bigger impact.

So make sure people know about these things. Tell them you're a thought leader. Tell them in multiple ways. Don't worry about repeating yourself. Because repetition is your friend. And the right people are ready to listen.

[BEN GIOIA IS THE IDEAL SPEAKER OR TRAINER FOR YOUR NEXT EVENT]

Dear Event or Meeting Planner,

I know that planning a meeting, event, or training is like being a leader. In today's economy, getting a return on your investment is more important than ever. And doing it in a way that brings value to everyone is a win-win.

That's why **my talks are designed to inspire and deliver value to your audience...** so they can discover how to be better leaders and communicators, and make a bigger impact with their business or in their organization.

For your attendees to reach their best, it's the inside game that leads to the outside win. **I help your audience realize that each one of them is a visionary, a leader, a game changer** (regardless of their profession or position)... whether they're influencing one person, leading a team of 10, or transforming the lives of 10,000!

As a highly in-demand speaker and bestselling author, I've presented to audiences around the country, around the world, and on the web... ranging from intimate groups of 10, to events with 500+ attendees.

I look forward to speaking with you soon! When you contact me, remember to ask how **you can get 100 free books** for your event! InfluenceWithAHeart.com/speaking

Cheers,

Ben

Chapter 4: Influencing Yourself: Mindfulness, Meditation, Innovation, and Other Success Habits

Thought
Leadership

Influence
WITH A HEART™

Empathy   Story

Summary

1. Meditation and mindfulness offer a wealth of proven results for individuals and organizations, including: increased productivity, more innovation, better engagement, improved resiliency, greater happiness, higher performance, decreased absenteeism, better communication, improved health and wellbeing, and greater profitability.

2. Many **entrepreneurs, visionaries, businesses, and organizations** — including Google, General Mills, Aetna, Goldman Sachs, Intel, Apple, Nike, Yahoo, Liberty Mutual, Deutsche Bank, and HBO — make mindfulness and/or meditation a key component their business.

3. Meditation and mindfulness can increase innovation, by helping you be more receptive to ideas and insights while cultivating your ability to engage with what's happening in a more focused, vibrant, and nonjudgemental way.

4. Part of **achieving your goals and dreams** comes from success habits like optimizing your morning, your day, and how you do your work. It's just as important to remember that success also comes from learning how to keep letting go.

Mindfulness and Meditation: Good For You, For Your Business, and For The World

A wealth of academic, scientific, and anecdotal evidence indicate that meditation and mindfulness practices help millions of people on multiple levels — physical, emotional, mental, psychological, and spiritual — every single day.

Many successful organizations of all sizes are seeing the **benefits of mindfulness and meditation:** greater happiness, increased productivity, more innovation, better engagement, and higher performance, just to name a few.

I've spent over 13 years studying and practicing mindfulness and meditation. I have an understanding of both the metaphysical and scientific components of mindfulness and empathy from reading countless books, studying with different teachers, having a daily practice, and being on silent meditation retreats for a total of 88 days (and counting).

In 2005, I created an online mindfulness and meditation program for people with ALS (Lou Gehrig's disease), their loved ones, and caregivers. It was called "Mindfulness for People With ALS and The People Who Love and Care For Them."

I developed this program for the Golden West Chapter of the ALS Association (which serves more than 50% of the people in California who are living with the disease).

What I discovered, was that mindfulness wasn't just for people with ALS and their families. It's also **a powerful tool for caregivers, doctors, social workers, scientists, and other people** who are working to cure ALS and improve people's quality of life.

I'm happy to share that I was honored with an "Excellence In Patient Services" Award from the National Office of The ALS Association. I was then **invited to present my program nationally** to Chapter leaders (through an online training).

It's been a delight to see that in the following years, more and more people and organizations are bringing mindfulness and meditation into the workplace.

Especially for businesses or organizations that help people with tough challenges (like ALS), mindfulness and meditation can be powerful supports in helping to make their leaders and employees happier and more resilient, especially in such difficult circumstances and situations.

I'm so happy to be able to leave such a powerful, positive legacy with the organization, and to keep helping people.

Meditation and Mindfulness for Entrepreneurs, Leaders, and Visionaries

More and more businesses are bringing meditation and mindfulness practices into the workplace because they:

1. Help make communication better;

2. Support employee's happiness and health while increasing loyalty and decreasing absenteeism; and

3. Improve clarity, focus, productivity, profitability, and contribute to growth.

If you do a quick search on the web, you'll find articles on CNN Money, Forbes, Huffington Post, Bloomberg Business — as well as multiple, reputable academic sources — about meditation and mindfulness and how they **contribute to business success and happiness.**

These practices can help entrepreneurs, executives, visionaries, and leaders be:

1. Better aligned with their highest purpose;

2. Flexible, adaptive, responsive, and resilient with what's happening and changing around them;

3. More effective in their thinking, decisions, and ability to create and share value; and

4. More understanding of themselves and (as a result), more confident, capable, and authentic.

As for me, I've been sitting meditation and doing mindfulness practices regularly for more than 13 years. **I couldn't live without them.** Let me rephrase: I wouldn't live without them.

I find meditation and mindfulness to be incredibly beneficial for:

1. Keeping me healthy (mentally, physically, emotionally);

2. Being more flexible, creative, and innovative;

3. Reducing anxiety, stress, doubt, and worry;

4. Dealing with physical and emotional pain;

5. Managing grief, impatience, and anger;

6. Navigating the unknown in a rapidly changing world;

7. Supporting this amazing, challenging, delightful adventure that is both my business and my life.

How I Discovered Mindfulness, The Hard Way

I once trekked through the Himalayas for 9 days, for 6 to 8 hours each day (at 12,000+ feet elevation). Every other day, we'd cross a high pass (16,000+ feet elevation). For the first few days, **I wanted to kill the guy** who just fixed my boots. Then, I wanted to hug him.

I'd already been living in Leh, Ladakh, India for a month. I was staying with a family and working on a farm, at 12,000+ feet. (Ladakh is the northernmost part of India, part of the Tibetan plateau, on the Silk Road, and has a mix of Tibetan, Muslim, and Hindu cultures.)

I was *almost* acclimatized to the elevation. I was *almost* able to get through a full day of harvesting barley without feeling totally wiped out, from the lack of oxygen.

I learned a lot about **being grateful...** simply for being able to take in enough air to survive.

When my farm stay ended, I planned a 9 day trek through the Himalayas with a small group of friends. As we were getting ready, I took at look at my boots. They were in terrible shape, especially the soles.

They were worn down... smooth... which didn't bode well for trekking through rocky/snowy/icy/wet terrain. And nobody in India (at least in Leh) sells size 13 boots. (The first store owner that I asked, actually laughed out loud.)

So I walked around the small city of Leh (pop. 25,000) looking for a cobbler. I found one whose shop was literally him: his tools and materials set up on the curb.

I asked if he could fix the soles. He said yes, explaining that he'd replace them with a strip of airplane tire rubber. So the result would be a sole that still looked smooth.

But since it was **airplane tire rubber,** it was incredibly tacky (as in sticky) and would do the trick. So I walked away, happy to know that I found an answer.

I came back the next day to pick up my boots. The work was superb, and now I was all set to hike with airplane wheels under my feet.

Then came the upsell.

The cobbler offered to fix the other parts of my boots that needed help (but in my mind weren't critical — it was only the soles that I cared about).

He pointed out some spots where the seams were separating, a broken aglet, and a rip at the back... where the boots were touching my Achilles tendon.

So, being grateful for his good work and since I was already planning to give him money in exchange for services, I said yes… especially because I could see that he was adding value to our exchange. (And **psychologically, once you say, "yes"** it's easier to say, "yes" again.)

Back again to the cobbler the next day… and it looked like my shoes were newer, shinier, and even more worthy of my first trek through the Himalayas. I felt like I'd made a good investment in gear that I absolutely needed for my upcoming adventure.

Then we started trekking: 4 donkeys, 3 friends, 2 Tibetan guides, and 1 horse. And after about 45 minutes into day 1… of a 6-8 hour day… of a 9 day trek… my Achilles **tendons started to hurt.** Both of them.

First, I thought it was my hiking socks, so I kept adjusting them. Then, I thought my boots were too tight. So I kept adjusting them.

Then, I took off my boots to discover what was really happening.

The cobbler had fixed the back of both boots… and in doing so, left a little lump of material that had been rubbing against my tendons, for almost 2 hours now.

The only thing I could do was take my knife and cut the lumps of material out. <u>But the damage was already done</u>.

Two tremendous blisters, a long mountainous trek ahead, and an incredible amount of **anger and self-judgment** for saying, "yes" to the upsell. I covered the blisters with moleskin, put the boots back on, and started walking.

I once heard Stedman Graham (business leader and spouse of Oprah Winfrey) say that winning means that you keep getting up every time you fall.

For me, winning meant taking one step (ouch!)… and then the next (ouch!)… and then the next (ouch, ouch, OUCH!)… **for minutes, hours, and days after days after days…** along the rocky terrain, over the tops of mountains (from 12,000' to 16,000' every other day), and back down slippery slopes. Ouch. Ouch. Ouch. Ouch!

On about day 3, I had a revelation. The ouch(!) of every single step (although it hurt like hell) gave me a gift. It anchored me to the present, to nearly every single moment of that entire trek.

I couldn't space out or become distracted because of the consistent, ongoing stabs of pain.

No, the pain was not fun. But being present was a gift.

I got to witness every beautiful mountain peak, every cloud, every rock that I passed. (If you've never seen the Tibetan Plateau, it is a true wonder of this Earth.)

I was alive and aware, wholly and completely, in every moment.

There was no tomorrow. No yesterday.

Just right now, right here.

The world was complete. I felt complete. And I was completely part of the world around me.

Thanks to that Ladakhi cobbler and his upsell, I finally understood something important.

The only real time is right here, right now. It's not yesterday (because it's gone) and it's not tomorrow (because there's no guarantee you'll get there).

Life is right now.

In the words of a whole bunch of wise folks:

"The past is history, the future's a mystery, today is a gift... and that's why it's called the present."

The Connections Among Mindfulness, Meditation, and Innovation

The benefits of mindfulness and meditation create the **perfect opportunity for innovation...** for individuals as well as organizations.

This is why companies like Google, General Mills, Aetna, Goldman Sachs, Intel, Apple, Nike, Yahoo, Deutsche Bank, HBO, and many others make mindfulness and/or meditation a key component their business.

Mindfulness and meditation stimulate the neocortex (the most evolved part of your brain), improve emotional intelligence, and reduce the "fight or flight" reaction that comes from your reptilian brain.

More mindfulness and meditation help you become less fixated and locked-in to your own biases and ideas. This is where innovation can happen.... when you're present, relaxed, aware, and open to possibility.

You'll be more receptive to ideas and insights while cultivating your ability to engage with what's happening in a more focused, vibrant, and nonjudgemental way. This "blank canvas" is an open space where something truly new and innovative can emerge, transforming your business and transforming the world.

Mindfulness, Leadership, and Bacon

[Disclaimer: These days, I don't eat meat or fish. However, in my earlier life, I did… and I sure loved bacon! So when a client recently asked me to describe mindfulness in a fun and accessible way, this is what came through. (If you don't like bacon, feel free to substitute another favorite food!)]

"Bacon!"

Do you remember that moment?

Let me take you there…

You feel a flutter of excitement in your belly as you hand your menu back to the server.

Bacon is coming.

You know it.

And you can already smell it.

You're aware of yourself as you look around at your surroundings — and at the other diners — as they eat breakfast.

You take a few, deep, nourishing breaths as you recognize some familiar faces. It's nice to see people you know.

As you hear the sounds of forks and knives gently hitting the plates nearby, it's clear that many people already have their bacon.

Bacon!

You notice a twinge of jealousy toward the other patrons, as well as impatience at your server (and the cook that you can't see) because you don't have your bacon... yet.

Then you acknowledge that sometimes your mind just churns out stories like these... and you don't need to "buy in" to the noisy, negative, incessant chit-chat.

You also realize that you're happy, because you know what it's like to experience, enjoy, and be grateful for the gift of bacon.

And... it's coming soon!

Now you can feel grumbling in your stomach.

So you take a moment, take a few deep breaths, and then smile...

Because the kitchen door just opened, and here comes bacon! Your mouth starts watering because you know the salty magic that's about to dazzle your palate....

So you offer thanks (and perhaps a little affirmation or prayer) for all of the great things in your life. Like bacon.

And then, you take a bite.

"Bacon!"

• • •

The preceding "bacon experience" is one way of describing mindfulness in action.

It doesn't mean that eating bacon = practicing mindfulness.

Nor does it mean that you MUST eat bacon... to be mindful.

It does mean you have the opportunity to practice mindfulness in every moment of your day (and get the benefits) at work and home, no matter what you're doing.

Wikipedia describes mindfulness as "... the intentional, accepting, and non-judgmental focus of one's attention on the emotions, thoughts, and sensations occurring in the present moment… "

The bacon experience offers these 10 examples of mindfulness:

1. Intentionally remembering an event/experience.

2. The present-moment physical awareness of yourself:
   a. via the sensations in your belly;
   b. the movement of your arm as you give the menu to the server; and
   c. the feeling of your body in contact with your seat.

3. Acknowledging a piece of information (bacon is coming).

4. Recognizing that you're anticipating an event (bacon is coming).

5. Being cognizant that you're smelling bacon.

6. Breathing… and knowing that you're doing it, as you're doing it.

7. Your awareness of yourself, your physical surroundings, ambient sounds, people around you, and feeling good because it's nice to see folks you know.

8. Remembering that your mind is a "thought factory" that pumps out a lot of noise (on top of, and in spite of, your wisdom and insights).

9. Offering gratitude to honor and acknowledge your blessings.

10. Being present… as you take your first bite.

What Comes Next?

After reading this…

• Some people go out for breakfast (regardless of the time of day) or make a BLT as quickly as possible.

• Others consider how they can bring more mindfulness and meditation into their communication, into their leadership, and into their lives.

What comes next for you?

Creating Success by Telling Yourself A Story

Everything that humans create begins in the mind and the heart: inspiration and insight... coupled with passion, intention, and the desire to bring things to life.

Put another way, what we think, say, and do creates our reality (in that order).

Uncountable numbers of scientists, leaders, athletes, spiritual masters, and high performers have proven this.

That's why so many **people who are committed to achieving their goals and dreams** dedicate time, energy, and intention to envisioning and affirming success.

Whether it's winning a gold medal, public speaking, self-healing, or just relaxing, the power of affirmative thinking, imagination, and visualization is astounding.

So I want to invite you into a brief imagination and visioning exercise (5 steps).

1. **Start** by taking a couple of deep breaths. Take a few moments to connect to your unique sense of purpose.

2. **Imagine** you've succeeded in every way you want (don't limit yourself).

3. **Feel,** in your heart and body, what that will do for you, your business, and the people you serve!

4. **Hold** that beautiful, powerful vision — and the feeling of the future you want — in your awareness for 2 or 3 breaths.

5. **Now, create your story** and visualize what you want to happen, happening successfully… (whether in the next 3 minutes, the next 3 months, or the next 3 years).

Whether you're preparing to make an offer, learn a skill, play a game of tennis, or follow your morning ritual… imagine yourself doing it (successfully) BEFORE you do it. Because what you do AND what you think about doing — are the same thing — as far as your brain is concerned.

This is why Olympic athletes invest lots time imagining themselves winning the gold.

Think of a high diver. Not only does she picture herself making the perfect dive and landing in the water without making a splash…

She also pictures herself at the moment the gold medal is being placed around her neck, and can she hear the resounding applause from the audience as a tear rolls down her cheek…

Your brain functions the same way. You can visualize your own success. It works best when you use as many of your 5 senses as possible... and make sure to add lots of emotion!

<u>I invite you to take 60 seconds, and try it out right now</u>.

1. What's something that you want to achieve?

2. When you're imagining it, what do you see?

3. What do you hear?

4. What do you taste or smell?

5. What can you feel?

6. What are **the emotions underneath,** as you're imagining yourself experiencing success, reaching your goals, or achieving your dreams?

7. How do you picture yourself celebrating your success?

Pretty cool, huh? You're literally **re-mapping your brain and rewiring your subconscious mind.**

Now that you see how easy it is, here are 3 great times during your day for visualizing success.

Influence With A Heart   by Ben Gioia

You can visualize your success for one, 5, or 15+ minutes. Remember, there's an important perspective to keep in mind here: 5 minutes = 1/3 of 1% of your day.

That's only 0.35% of your entire day... to craft success, to make a bigger impact, and create the life you want.

1. **Before bed.** Look back on what you've accomplished. Smile and feel satisfied. Then envision a successful day tomorrow.

2. **In the morning.** Visualize having a successful day, one where you do great work, serve lots of people, and have lots of fun! Imagine your day moving seamlessly from one pleasant experience to the next.

3. **Before each segment of your day.** Imagine quick, effective, enjoyable, and fulfilling success. Anticipate the challenges... and the solutions to move beyond them.

While visualizing your future is a powerful way to help you succeed — because you're imprinting your subconscious with the images of the future you want — you still want to spend the vast majority of your time here and now, in the present moment.

As you know, two great tools that can support you are meditation and mindfulness.

One Success Habit Made Famous,
Thanks To One Historical American President

I have a story for you, about a young man… who was alive more than 150 years ago.

That's the 1800s, as a matter of fact.

Back then, certain things hadn't been invented yet. There were no cellphones. Actually, there were no phones at all. (He died one year before the first phone call.)

There was no internet, of course.

But there was this certain young man.

He came from a poor family, and his mother died when he was a small child.

From her teaching and example, there were two important things he learned, remembered, and practiced in his life.

The first (which the mother is said to have shared with her family on her deathbed) was, **"Be good to one another."**

The second was **discipline.**

Now, this was not the kind of discipline that most people think of when they hear that word. This was not a punishment, a "time out," or "you're in trouble." This was the kind discipline which is the foundation of success.

It was the kind of discipline — that would create the thoughts, behaviors, and ultimately the habits — that helped this young man succeed. And he did truly amazing things.

According to some people, he's famous for saying this:

"If I had six hours to chop down a tree, I'd spend the first four hours sharpening the axe."

After you've let this quote sink in, take a moment and think about your week...

You go to work (or work from home), learn lots of new information, process new ideas, interact with different people, try to get in some exercise... and still have time to savor this gift of life, and spend time with the people you love. (And get plenty of sleep and eat right too.)

Are you actually able to do all that?

If the answer if "no," don't go beating yourself up. Maybe you just never learned how to sharpen your axe.

(At this point, you might be saying, "But I don't even HAVE an axe!")

That's okay.

Because the "axe" is your mind.

And you sharpen it by creating habits.

Good habits.

When you create (and maintain) good habits, lots of good things can happen for you, very quickly.

<u>Here are 3 of those good things:</u>

1. You can focus and pay attention to what you're doing for longer, so you stop getting distracted. This means you get more done than ever before, faster.

2. You have less stress and anxiety, sleep better, and feel healthier.

3. You achieve more with less effort and have more fun with what you're doing... so you can reach your biggest goals and dreams, while having the life you want today.

Are you ready to sharpen your axe?

If so, it's **simply a matter of learning one new habit,** and doing it each day.

Here's the one habit: Create a morning ritual that you love... and do it daily.

Your morning ritual sets the tone for success, as you care for your body, mind, and spirit. This is where you start sharpening the axe **so you can have an amazing day!**

Here's an example:

• Eating a healthy breakfast (15 minutes);

• Making your bed (2 minutes);

• Reading something inspiring (5 minutes);

• Drinking 16 ounces of water (3 minutes);

• Meditating (10 minutes); and

• Exercising (20 minutes).

• [Total: 55 minutes]

Imagine doing all of this before you even leave the house or start your work! How do you imagine your day will go?

<u>Important</u>: when you create your own morning ritual, do the same things in the same order, each day.

This will make it easier to do it... since you won't have to spend time or energy thinking or making choices.

You can save your energy and brain for **more innovation, successes, creativity,** and what will happen throughout the day... because you'll need it!

(Inspired by Hal Elrod's *Miracle Morning*.)

Oh, I almost forgot...

This young man, the one with the axe... in case you were still wondering...

That was Abraham Lincoln.

He kept sharpening his axe.

Look what he did, and how many people he impacted, in his lifetime and beyond...

Now imagine what your business and life will be like when you keep sharpening your axe!

Learning How To Keep Letting Go, So You Can Make The Impact You Want

The things we experience — with others, in the world around us, and with ourselves — are impacted by our interpretations, expectations, assumptions, intentions, beliefs, biology, principles, values, environment, associations, fears, and/or desires.

That's a lot of "noise" that can keep us from seeing the truth and the reality of the world around us and within ourselves.

For as much as we all must keep learning and understanding and discovering — there's as much, if not more, that **we need to unlearn and release** — so we can grow, succeed, and make a bigger positive impact in the world.

And so we can love who we are and what we're about, every single day.

Otherwise, our ability to make a bigger impact and live the life that we love is **limited by the roles, stories, and beliefs that have been handed to us**, rather than what we've discovered for ourselves.

Much of the wisdom, joy, and magic that shows up in our

lives... happens when we let things go.

Did you ever stop and think about all the learning that's happened in your life?

So much learning, so much information, so many experiences.

So many things, and some might be holding you back...

... from yourself, your greatness, your happiness, doing the work you love (and doing it on your own terms), and living your life the way you want to live it.

• It might be what you learned at school, and what you learned from your parents and friends.

• What (many of us) learned from television.

• There's what the internet teaches.

• What work teaches.

• What your mistakes and misperceptions teach.

• What debt and scarcity thinking teach.

• What religion and spirituality teach.

• What altered states of consciousness teach.

• What our spouses or partners teach.

• What our children teach.

• What our pets teach.

• What sickness, old age, and death teach.

That's a lot of teaching, from when you were young and very impressionable — to now, today: less impressionable, a bit wiser, and more discerning.

All of us have values and beliefs that we never chose for ourselves, but somehow they became a part of us.

And part of the business world.

And that's usually what holds us back.

So what's one thing you can let go of, right now?

From there, what do you want to cultivate more of… as you take your business (and your life) to the next level?

What are you going to do for yourself, for your business, and your life, so you can make a bigger impact?

Wrapping It All Up

In those fateful 72 hours in India, when I almost died 4 times, my life flashed before my eyes.

Because of that, I'd like to leave you with an important thought:

• **When your flashes before your eyes, make sure it's something you want to watch.**

Because… you're amazing and there's nobody like you!

You already impact and transform people's businesses and their lives — through what you offer.

Are you ready to turn up the volume? Are you ready to be a better leader, be a better communicator, and make a bigger impact?

The path is simple. It all starts when you communicate with more influence… by using more empathy, story, and thought leadership.

• Why? Your clients, customers, colleagues, and/or audience need to get inspired and excited about who you are and what you offer, so they can take action that's good for them and good for you.

• They must understand that you are an authentic leader, expert, authority, or thought leader who understands and cares about them.

(And then they will tell others about you and how you've impacted their business or life.)

The fastest, simplest way to inspire and influence more people (ethically) is by using more empathy, story, and thought leadership every time you communicate.

You can do this anytime, anywhere, with anyone: in person, online, onstage, on the phone, in a training, in a video, during a speech, or in a meeting. Whether you're communicating with 1, 10, or 10,000 people, it works.

So, think about all the people who need what you offer, and are waiting for you right now… Imagine the impact that you're going to make…

Realize that you now have a powerful framework and an array of strategies and approaches to make it happen!

*(I promised I would teach you that, in this book.
And that's what I've shared. Thanks for reading.)*

THE CORE TEACHING: When you communicate with more influence you will inspire more people and make an even bigger impact. This means using more empathy, story, and thought leadership. Here's the summary:

1. Empathy gives you the opportunity to see the world through another person's eyes and connect with them from a place of authenticity, integrity, and service.

2. Stories reach people's hearts as well as their minds. So your stories create inspiration... by creating an emotional experience for your reader or listener.

3. Thought leadership positions you as a reliable source of information, insight, and as a go-to person who is successful, can replicate success, and can teach others how to be successful. It's your legacy, and how you keep making an impact, long after you're gone.

In conclusion, by using more empathy, story, and thought leadership (communicating with more influence) 7 wonderful things happen:

1. You'll be positioned as an expert, authority, or thought leader who people know, like, and trust.

(So when people invest in your training, service, product, or program — or get behind you and your vision — they will be even more invested in their success, and therefore your success.)

2. You'll inspire and invite people to change their thoughts — so they can choose to change their behaviors — and transform their business or their life.

3. You're able to offer unique perspectives, tools, and techniques, so the people you reach can be more successful and make a bigger impact in their world.

4. **More people will say, "yes"** to your ideas, vision, message, products, and/or services… whether it's your clients, customers, audience, colleagues, partners, employees, stakeholders, team, and/or the media.

5. **More people will take action.** (Because more people will have the opportunity to have their business or life transformed by what you offer.)

6. You'll create influence, with a heart. Because you'll connect people to each other and build a bridge from your vision — to their goals and dreams — so **everyone will benefit from the gifts and insights that you offer to the world.**

7. When you communicate with more influence, the people you impact will become your fans, clients, tribe, customers, community, referral network, affiliate partners, and more — bringing a flood of new and repeat

business to your door — so you can make an even bigger impact!

That's what Influence With A Heart™ is all about.

Thanks for reading!

May what you've learned — and what has inspired you — be an ongoing support for your success!

I also want to offer you so much gratitude and respect for doing all of the amazing things you do in this world!

Cheers,

Ben

P.S.

If you're ready to be an even better leader, be more successful, and help more people, connect with me today at InfluenceWithAHeart.com/contact

Page 144

Acknowledgements

As often as I can throughout every single day...

I'm so happy and grateful for all the blessings I have and all the blessings I'm receiving.

I'm grateful for everything that supports my life and makes it possible for me to make my unique impact in the world.

May all beings realize their greatness, act with more compassion, help more people, and live in freedom.

• • •

[To everyone who helped in the physical, digital, spiritual, and inspirational production of this book: Alia Shah, my family (so much gratitude), Haisam Hussein (graphics), Zeke Kossover (cover photo), Johan del Barrio (cover design), Rainbow Xue, Farzad Wafapoor, and Nicola Grace (for seeing what I can do when given a platform to do it), George Schofield, James Malinchak, and Lou D'Alo (for mentoring me over the years), Intel (for the font Clear Sans), Christian Robertson (for the font Roboto), Roman Shamin (for the font Hattori Hanzo), and Amazon.com (for helping to put the power of publishing into the hands of the people)...thanks!]

www.ingramcontent.com/pod-product-compliance
Lightning Source LLC
Chambersburg PA
CBHW062007200326

41519CB00017B/4713